# THE *Lyric* LIBRARY

# Country

## Complete Lyrics for 200 Songs

D1599171

HAL•LEONARD

Other books in *The Lyric Library*:

Broadway Volume I
Broadway Volume II
Christmas
Classic Rock
Contemporary Christian
Early Rock 'n' Roll
Love Songs
Pop/Rock Ballads

ISBN 0-634-04509-1

Library of Congress cataloguing-in-publication data has been applied for.

Visit Hal Leonard Online at
**www.halleonard.com**

# Preface

Songs have an uncanny ability to burrow deep into our gray matter, sometimes lying dormant for years or decades before something pings them back into our consciousness. All kinds of songs reside in there, more than we can count—not just songs we love and intentionally memorized and have sung again and again, but songs we once heard in passing, songs that form a soundtrack to significant people and places and moments in our lives, and even (or especially) songs that drive us crazy, like the chirping TV jingle that still won't let go years after the product it plugged has disappeared from the shelves.

Most of the time, though, our memories of songs are frustratingly incomplete unless we actively maintain them. The first verse and chorus that we blare out in the shower or at the jam session degenerates into mumbled lines, disconnected phrases, and bits and pieces inadvertently lifted from other songs. And, of course, there's the likelihood that what we *do* remember is riddled with mondegreens, or misheard lyrics. In these pages you'll find many opportunities to bring a little more completeness and accuracy to your country repertoire, as well as to rediscover a nearly forgotten gem, wallow in nostalgia, or just browse through some prominent examples of the songwriter's craft.

The songs collected here span many decades, from Eddy Arnold's setting of the venerable mountain theme "Will the Circle Be Unbroken" and Hank Williams' classic anthems of lonely hearts and honky tonkin' right on through the soaring harmonies of the Dixie Chicks and Alan Jackson's September 11 memorial, "Where Were You (When the World Stopped Turning)." For all the changes in American life over the decades, country songwriters have returned again and again to a few thematic wells. So in this collection we find many celebrations of rural life ("Jambalaya," "Thank God I'm a Country Boy"), lots of tears in beers and cheating spouses, miles and miles of restless rambling, and the kind of folksy humor that gives us such memorable only-in-country-music titles as "Here's a Quarter (Call Someone Who Cares)," "My Baby Thinks He's a Train," and "All My Ex's Live in Texas."

This consistency makes sense considering that one of country music's perennial themes is precisely hanging onto your roots and values as modern life spins you in unpredictable new directions. "Even if the whole world has forgotten," as Hugh Prestwood put it, "the song remembers when."

# Contents

# Country

# Abilene

Words and Music by Lester Brown, John D. Loudermilk and Bob Gibson

recorded by George Hamilton IV, Sonny James

*Refrain:*
Abilene, Abilene,
Prettiest town I've ever seen.
Women down there don't treat you mean
In Abilene, my Abilene.

I sit alone most ev'ry night,
Watch those trains pull out of sight.
Don't I wish that they were carrying me
Back to Abilene, my Abilene.

*Refrain*

Crowded city, there ain't nothin' free;
Nothing in this town for me.
Wish to the Lord that I could be
In Abilene, sweet Abilene.

*Repeat All*

# Act Naturally

Words and Music by Vonie Morrison and Johnny Russell

recorded by Buck Owens


They're gonna put me in the movies,
They're gonna make a big star out of me.
We'll make a film about a man that's sad and lonely,
And all I gotta do is act nat'rally.

Well, I'll bet you I'm gonna be a big star,
Might win an Oscar, you can never tell.
The movie's gonna make me a big star
'Cause I can play the part so well.

Well, I hope you come and see me in the movies,
Then I know that you will plainly see
The biggest fool that ever hit the big time.
And all I gotta do is act nat'rally.

We'll make the scene about a man that's sad and lonely
And beggin' down upon his bended knee.
I'll play the part, but I won't need rehearsin';
All I have to do is act nat'rally.

*Repeat Verse 2 and 3*

# Ain't Goin' Down ('Til the Sun Comes Up)

Words and Music by Kim Williams, Garth Brooks and Kent Blazy

recorded by Garth Brooks

Six o'clock on Friday evening,
Mama doesn't know she's leaving
'Til she hears the screen door slamming,
Rubber squealing, gears a-jammin,
Local country station
Just a-blaring on the radio.
Pick him up at seven
And they're heading to the rodeo.
Mama's on the front porch,
Screaming out a warning:
"Girl, you'd better get your red head
Back in bed before the morning."

Nine o'clock, the show is ending,
But the fun is just beginning.
She knows he's anticipating,
But she's gonna keep him waiting.
First a bite to eat,
And then they're heading to the honky-tonk.
But loud crowds and line dancing
Just ain't what they really want.
Drive out to the boondocks
And park down by the creek,
Where it's George Strait
'Til real late
And dancing cheek to cheek.

*Refrain:*
They ain't going down 'til the sun comes up,
Ain't giving in 'til they get enough.
Going 'round the world in a pick-up truck.
Ain't going down 'til the sun comes up.

Ten 'til twelve it's wine and dancing.
Midnight starts the hard romancing.
One o'clock that truck is rocking.
Two is coming, still no stopping.
Break to check the clock at three.
They're right at where they want to be
And four o'clock get up and going.
Five o'clock that rooster's crowing.
Hey. Yeah, they…

*Refrain*

Six o'clock on Saturday,
Her folks don't know he's on his way.
The stalls are clean, the horses fed.
They say she's grounded 'til she's dead.
Well, here he comes around the bend,
Slowing down. She's jumping in.
Hey, Mom, your daughter's gone.
And there they go again.
Hey.

*Refrain Twice*

# All My Ex's Live in Texas

Words and Music by Lyndia J. Shafer and Sanger D. Shafer

recorded by George Strait

*Refrain:*
All my ex's live in Texas,
And Texas is a place I'd dearly love to be.
But all my ex's live in Texas,
And that's why I hang my hat in Tennessee.

Rosanna's down in Texarkana; wanted me to push her broom.
And sweet Ilene's in Abilene; she forgot I hung the moon.
And Allison in Galveston somehow lost her sanity.
And Dimples who now lives in Temple's got the law lookin' for me.

*Refrain*

I remember that old Frio River where I learned to swim,
And it brings to mind another time where I wore my welcome thin.
My transcendental meditation, I go there each night.
But I always come back to myself long before daylight.

All my ex's live in Texas,
And Texas is a place I'd dearly love to be.
But all my ex's live in Texas.
Therefore I reside in Tennessee.

Some folks think I'm hiding.
It's been rumored that I died.
But I'm alive and well in Tennessee.

# All the Gold in California

Words and Music by Larry Gatlin

recorded by The Gatlin Brothers

*Refrain:*
All the gold in California
Is in the bank in the middle of Beverly Hills
In somebody else's name.
So if you're dreamin' about California,
It don't matter at all where you've played before.
California's a brand-new game.

Tryin' to be a hero, winding up a zero,
Can scar a man forever right down to your soul.
Living on the spotlight can kill a man outright
'Cause everything that glitters is not gold.

*Refrain*

# Always on My Mind

Words and Music by Wayne Thompson, Mark James and Johnny Christopher

recorded by Willie Nelson, Elvis Presley and various other artists

Maybe I didn't treat you
Quite as good as I should have.
Maybe I didn't love you,
Quite as often as I should have;
Little things I should have said and done,
I just never took the time.

You were always on my mind;
You were always on my mind.

Tell me,
Tell me that your sweet love hasn't died.
Give me,
Give me one more chance to keep you satisfied, satisfied.

Maybe I didn't hold you,
All those lonely, lonely times;
And I guess I never told you
I'm so happy that you're mine.
If I made you feel second best,
Girl, I'm sorry I was blind.

You were always on my mind;
You were always on my mind.

# Amazed

Words and Music by Marv Green, Chris Lindsey and Aimee Mayo

recorded by Lonestar

Every time our eyes meet,
This feelin' inside me
Is almost more than I can take.
Baby, when you touch me,
I can feel how much you love me,
And it just blows me away.
I've never been this close to anyone or
  anything.
I can hear your thoughts.
I can see your dreams.

Refrain:
I don't know how you do what you do,
I'm so in love with you.
It just keeps gettin' better.
I wanna spend the rest of my life
With you by my side, forever and ever.
Every little thing that you do,
Baby, I'm amazed by you.

The smell of your skin,
The taste of your kiss,
The way you whisper in the dark.
Your hair all around me;
Baby, you surround me.
You touch every place in my heart.
Oh, it feels like the first time every time.
I wanna spend the whole night in your eyes.

*Refrain*

Every little thing that you do
I'm so in love with you.
It just keeps gettin' better.
I wanna spend the rest of my life
With you by my side forever and ever.
Every little thing that you do,
Oh, every little thing that you do,
Baby, I'm amazed by you.

# American Made

Words and Music by Bob DiPiero and Pat McManus

recorded by The Oak Ridge Boys

Seems ev'rything you buy these days has got a foreign name,
From the kind of car I drive to my video game.
I got a Nikon camera, a Sony color TV,
But the one that I love is from the USA and layin' next to me.

*Refrain:*
Oh, my baby's American made,
Born and bred in the USA,
From her silky long hair to her sexy long legs,
My baby is American made.

She looks good in her tight blue jeans she bought in Mexico,
And she loves wearin' French perfume ev'rywhere we go.
But when it comes to the lovin' part, one thing is true;
My baby's genuine USA, red, white, and blue.

*Refrain*

# Angel of the Morning

Words and Music by Chip Taylor

recorded by Juice Newton and various other artists

There'll be no strings to bind your hands,
Not if my love can't bind your heart.
And there's no need to take a stand,
For it was I who chose to start.
I see no need to take me home
I'm old enough to face the dawn.

Just call me angel of the morning (angel).
Just touch my cheek before you leave me, baby.
Just call me angel of the morning (angel),
Then slowly turn away from me.

Maybe the sun's light will be dim,
And it won't matter anyhow.
If morning's echo says we've sinned,
Well, it was what I wanted now.
And if we're victims of the night,
I won't be blinded by the light.

Just call me angel of the morning (angel).
Just touch my cheek before you leave me, baby.
Just call me angel of the morning (angel),
Then slowly turn away.

I won't beg you to stay with me,
Through the tears of the day, of the years.
Baby, baby, baby.

*Repeat and Fade:*
Just call me angel of the morning (angel).
Just touch my cheek before you leave me, baby.

# Another Sleepless Night

Words and Music by Rory Bourke and Charlie Black

recorded by Anne Murray

The nights have been so lonely
Since you went away.
I could not get to sleep,
Try as I may.

Still it looks like another sleepless night.
Oh, but darlin', that's all right,
Just as long as you're holdin' me tight.
Makin' love till the early mornin' light
Only whets our appetite.
This will be another sleepless night.
Hold me while the moon shines in through the window.
Let your love flow.
Hold me. We can orchestrate love's scenario with the radio.

And it looks like another sleepless night.
Oh, but darlin', that's all right,
Just as long as you're holdin' me tight.
Makin' love till the early mornin' light
Only whets our appetite.
This will be another sleepless night.
Hold me while the moon shines in through the window.
Let your love flow.
Hold me. We can orchestrate love's scenario with the radio.

# (Hey, Won't You Play) Another Somebody Done Somebody Wrong Song

Words and Music by Larry Butler and Chips Moman

recorded by B.J. Thomas

It's lonely out tonight
And the feelin' just got right
For a brand new love song,
Somebody done somebody wrong song.

*Refrain:*
Hey, won't you play
Another somebody done somebody wrong song,
And make me feel at home
While I miss my baby, while I miss my baby.

So play, play for me a sad melody,
So sad that it makes ev'rybody cry.
A real hurtin' song about a love that's gone wrong,
'Cause I don't wanna cry all alone.

*Refrain*

# Any Time

Words and Music by Herbert Happy Lawson

recorded by Eddy Arnold and various other artists

Any time you're feeling lonely,
Any time you're feeling blue,
Any time you feel downhearted,
That will prove your love for me is true.

Any time you're thinking 'bout me,
That's the time I'll be thinking of you,
So anytime you say you want me back again,
That's the time I'll come back home to you.

# Auctioneer

Words and Music by Leroy Van Dyke and Buddy Black

recorded by Leroy Van Dyke

*Spoken:*
Hey, well, all right, sir, here we go there, and what are ya gonna give for 'em.
I'm bid twenty-five, will ya gimme thirty, make it thirty, bid it to buy 'em at thirty dollars
on 'er, will ya gimme thirty, now five, who woulda bid it at five, five bid and now forty
dollars on 'er to buy 'em there...

There was a boy in Arkansas who wouldn't listen to his ma
When she told him that he should go to school.
He'd sneak away in the afternoon, take a little walk, and pretty soon
You'd find him at the local auction barn.
He'd stand and listen carefully, then pretty soon he began to see
How the auctioneer could talk so rapidly.
He said, "Oh my, it's do or die; I've got to learn that auction cry.
Gotta make my mark and be an auctioneer."

Twenty-five dollar bid and now thirty dollar, thirty,
Will you gimme thirty, make it thirty, bi-di-di-bom a thirty dollar,
Will you gimme thirty, who-da-da bi-da-da thirty dollar bid.
Thirty dollar bid and now thirty-five,
Will you gimme thirty-five to make it a thirty-five, to bi-da-da thirty-five,
Who woulda bid it at a thirty-five dollar bid.

As time went on he did his best, and all could see he didn't jest;
He practiced calling bids both night and day.
His pop would find him behind the barn just working up an awful storm
As he tried to imitate the auctioneer.
Then his pop said, "Son, we just can't stand to have a mediocre man
Sellin' things at auction using our good name.
I'll send you off to auction school; then you'll be nobody's fool.
You can take your place among the best."

Thirty-five dollar bid and now forty dollar, forty,
Will you gimme forty, make it forty, bi-di-di-bom a forty dollar,
Will you gimme forty, who-da-da bi-da-da forty dollar bid.
Forty dollar bid and now forty-five,
Will you gimme forty-five to make it a forty-five, to bi-da-da forty-five,
Who woulda bid it at a forty-five dollar bid.

So from that boy who went to school there grew a man who played it cool;
He came back home a full-fledged auctioneer.
Then the people came from miles around
Just to hear him make that rhythmic sound
That filled their hearts with such a happy cheer.
Then his fame spread out from shore to shore;
He had all he could do and more. Had to buy a plane to get around.
Now he's the tops in all the land. Let's pause to give that man a hand;
He's the best hillbilly auctioneer.

Forty-five dollar bid and now fifty dollar, fifty,
Will you gimme fifty, make it fifty, bi-di-di-bom a fifty dollar,
Will you gimme fifty, who-da-da bi-da-da fifty dollar bid.
Fifty dollar bid and now fifty-five,
Will you gimme fifty-five to make it a fifty-five, to bi-da-da fifty-five.
I sold that hog for a fifty-five dollar bid.

*Spoken:*
Hey, well all right, sir, open the gate and let 'em out and walk 'em, boys! Here we come
with lot number 29 in, what'd ya gonna give for 'em? I'm bid twenty-five, will ya gimme
thirty, make it thirty, bid it to buy 'em at thirty dollars on 'er, will you gimme thirty
dollars on 'er, now five, thirty-five, and now the forty dollars on 'er, will you gimme forty,
make it forty, now five, forty-five and now the fifty dollars on 'er, will you gimme fifty, now
five, fifty-five, and now the sixty dollars on 'er, will you gimme sixty, make it sixty, now
five, who'd-a bid it at sixty dollars on 'er to buy 'em there...

# Baby I Lied

Words and Music by Rafe VanHoy, Rory Michael Bourke and Deborah Allen

recorded by Deborah Allen

Did I say I wouldn't be hurt
If our love just didn't work?
Did I say that I'd be okay
If you said good-bye?
And did I promise you
I could take it if we were through,
And forget about these feelings inside?

*Refrain:*
(Baby, I lied) When I told you I could walk away
(Baby, I lied) And forget about the love we made.
I swear on my heart,
I was telling the truth at the time.
Baby, I lied. Baby, I lied.

And did I ever tell myself
I could always find someone else?
Did I say if you left today
It'd be no surprise?
Did I ever leave any doubt
I could hold up if you walked out?
I know I told you that I could survive.

*Refrain*

And now that I can see you
Walking out of my life, saying good-bye,
I realize baby, baby, baby,

(Baby, I lied) Don't believe a word I said before.
(Baby, I lied) Believe me when I say I love you more.
When I said I was sure
I could live without you by my side,
Baby, I lied. Baby, I lied.

# Big City

Words and Music by Merle Haggard and Dean Holloway

recorded by Merle Haggard

I'm tired of this dirty old city,
Entirely too much work and never enough play.
And I'm tired of these dirty old sidewalks;
Think I'll walk off my steady job today.

*Refrain:*
Turn me loose, set me free,
Somewhere in the middle of Montana,
And gimme all I've got comin' to me.
And keep your retirement and your so-called social security.
Big city, turn me loose and set me free.

Been workin' ev'ry day since I was twenty,
Haven't got a thing to show for anything I've done.
There's folks who never work, and they've got plenty;
Think it's time some guys like me had some fun.

*Refrain*

# Big Bad John

Words and Music by Jimmy Dean

recorded by Jimmy Dean

Every morning at the mine you could see him arrive,
He stood six-foot-six and weighed two-forty-five.
Kinda broad at the shoulder and narrow at the hip,
And everybody knew you didn't give no lip to Big John!

*Refrain:*
Big John, Big John,
Big Bad John, Big John.

Nobody seemed to know where John called home,
He just drifted into town and stayed all alone.
He didn't say much, a-kinda quiet and shy,
And if you spoke at all, you just said "hi" to Big John!

Somebody said he came from New Orleans,
Where he got in a fight over a Cajun queen.
And a crashing blow from a huge right hand
Sent a Lousiana fellow to the Promised Land. Big John!

*Refrain*

Then came the day at the bottom of the mine
When a timber cracked and the men started crying.
Miners were praying and hearts beat fast,
And everybody thought that they'd breathed their last, 'cept John.

Through the dust and the smoke of this man-made hell
Walked a giant of a man that the miners knew well.
Grabbed a sagging timber, gave out with a groan,
And like a giant oak tree, just stood there alone. Big John!

And with all of his strength he gave a mighty shove;
Then a miner yelled out, "There's a light up above!"
And twenty men scrambled from a would-be grave,
Now there's only one left down there to save—Big John!

With jacks and timbers they started back down,
Then came that rumble way down in the ground,
And smoke and gas belched out of that mine,
Everybody knew it was the end of the line for Big John!

*Refrain*

Now they never reopened that worthless pit,
They just placed a marble stand in front of it.
These few words are written on that stand:
"At the bottom of this mine lies a big, big man. Big John!"

*Refrain*

# Bird Dog

Words and Music by Boudleaux Bryant

recorded by The Everly Brothers

Johnny is a joker (he's a bird),
A very funny joker (he's a bird),
But when he jokes my honey (he's a dog),
His jokin' ain't so funny (what a dog).
Johnny is the joker that's a-tryin' to steal my baby (he's a bird dog).

*Refrain:*
Hey, bird dog, get away from my quail.
Hey, bird dog, you're on the wrong trail.
Bird dog, you'd better leave my lovey dove alone.
Hey, bird dog, get away from my chick.
Hey, bird dog, you'd better get away quick.
Bird dog, you'd better find a chicken little of your own.

Johnny sings a love song (like a bird),
He sings the sweetest love song (you ever heard).
But when he sings to my gal (what a howl),
To me he's just a wolf dog (on the prowl).
Johnny wants to fly away and puppy love my baby (he's a bird dog).

*Refrain*

Johnny kissed the teacher (he's a bird).
He tiptoed up to reach her (he's a bird).
Well, he's the teacher's pet now (he's a dog).
What he wants he can get now (what a dog).
He even made the teacher let him sit next to my baby (he's a bird dog).

*Refrain*

# Blessed Are the Believers

Words and Music by Rory Bourke, Charlie Black and Sandy Pinkard

recorded by Anne Murray

Rain in the sky,
A tear in my eye,
Static on the radio.
The long night's begun
With dinner for one.
You said you'd never go.

*Refrain:*
Blessed are the believers.
They shall inherit a heartache.
Believing in you, babe,
That was my greatest heartbreak.
Blessed are all the left behind,
For their hearts shall one day mend.
When love and those same sweet lies
Make us believers again.

Cold coffee cup,
Sun coming up,
Sleep is a distant dream.
Something you said
Rolls 'round in my head,
Something that you didn't mean.

*Refrain*

# Blue

Words and Music by Bill Mack

recorded by LeAnn Rimes

Blue, oh, so lonesome for you.
Why can't you be blue over me?
Blue, oh, so lonesome for you.
Tears fill my eyes till I can't see.

Three o'clock in the morning here am I,
Sitting here so lonely,
So lonesome I could cry.
Blue, oh, so lonesome for you.
Why can't you be blue for me?

Now that it's over, I realized
Those weak words you whispered
Were nothing but lies.
Blue, oh, so lonesome for you.
Why can't you be blue over me?
Why can't you be blue over me?

# Blue Bayou

Words and Music by Roy Orbison and Joe Melson

recorded by Roy Orbison, Linda Ronstadt

I feel so bad, I've got a worried mind;
I'm so lonesome all the time,
Since I left my baby behind on Blue Bayou.
Saving nickels, saving dimes;
Working 'til the sun don't shine;
Looking forward to happier times on Blue Bayou.

I'm going back someday,
Come what may, to Blue Bayou,
Where you sleep all day
And the catfish play on Blue Bayou.
All those fishing boats with their sails afloat;
If I could only see
That familiar sunrise through sleepy eyes,
How happy I'd be.

Go to see my baby again
And to be with some of my friends;
Maybe I'd be happy then on Blue Bayou.
Saving nickels, saving dimes;
Working 'til the sun don't shine;
Looking forward to happier times on Blue Bayou.

I'm going back someday,
Gonna stay on Blue Bayou,
Where the folks are fine
And the world is mine on Blue Bayou.
Ah, that girl of mine by my side,
The silver moon and the evening tide,
Oh, some sweet day,
Gonna take away this hurtin' inside.

I'll never be blue;
My dreams come true
On Blue Bayou.

# Blue Eyes Crying in the Rain

Words and Music by Fred Rose

recorded by Willie Nelson

In the twilight glow I see her
Blue eyes crying in the rain.
As we kissed good-bye and parted
I knew we'd never meet again.

Love is like a dying ember.
Only memories remain.
Through the ages I'll remember
Blue eyes crying in the rain.

Now my hair has turned to silver.
All my life I've loved in vain.
I can see her star in heaven,
Blue eyes crying in the rain.

Someday when we meet up yonder,
We'll stroll hand in hand again
In a land that knows no parting,
Blue eyes crying in the rain.

# Blue Moon of Kentucky

Words and Music by Bill Monroe

recorded by Bill Monroe & His Blue Grass Boys, Elvis Presley, Patsy Cline and various other artists

Blue moon, blue moon, blue moon keep a-shinin' bright.
Blue moon keep on a-shinin' bright,
You're gonna bring-a me back-a my baby tonight;
Blue moon keep a-shinin' bright!

*Refrain:*
I said blue moon of Kentucky to keep on shining,
Shine on the one that's gone and left me blue.
Blue moon of Kentucky to keep on shining,
Shine on the one that's gone and left me blue.

Well, it was on one moonlit night,
Stars shinin' bright,
Whisper on high
Love said goodbye.

Blue moon of Kentucky keep on shining,
Shine on the one that's gone and left me blue.

*Refrain*

Well, it was on one moonlit night,
Stars shinin' bright,
Whisper on high,
Your lover said goodbye.

Blue moon of Kentucky keep on shinin'.
Shine on the one that's gone and left me blue.

# Bonaparte's Retreat

Words and Music by Redd Stewart and Pee Wee King

recorded by Glen Campbell, Pee Wee King

Met the girl I love
In a town way down in Dixie
'Neath the stars above.
She was the sweetest girl I ever did see.
So I took her in my arms
And told her of her many charms.
I kissed her while the fiddles played
The Bonaparte's Retreat.

All the world was bright
As I held her on that night.
And I heard her say,
"Please don't ever go away."
So I held her in my arms
And told her of her many charms.
I kissed her while the fiddles played
The Bonaparte's Retreat.

# Boot Scootin' Boogie

Words and Music by Ronnie Dunn

recorded by Brooks & Dunn

Out in the country past the city limits sign,
Well, there's a honky tonk near the county line.
The joint starts jumpin' ev'ry night when the sun goes down.
They got whiskey, women, music, and smoke.
It's where all the cowboy folk
Go to boot scootin' boogie.

I've got a good job, I work hard for my money.
When it's quittin' time, I hit the door runnin'.
I fire up my pickup truck and let the horses run.
I go flyin' down that highway to that hideaway
Stuck out in the woods,
To do the boot scootin' boogie.

*Refrain:*
Yeah, heel to toe, docie doe,
Come on, baby, let's go boot scootin'!
Woh, Cadillac, Blackjack, baby, meet me out back,
We're gonna boogie.
Oh, get down, turn around, go to town,
Boot scootin' boogie.

The bartender asks me, says, "Son, what will it be?"
I want a shot at the redhead yonder lookin' at me.
The dance floor's hoppin', and it's hotter than the Fourth of July.
I see outlaws, in-laws, crooks, and straights,
All out makin' it shake,
Doin' the boot scootin' boogie.

*Refrain*

I said, get down, turn around, go to town,
Boot scootin' boogie.
Woh, get down, turn around, go to town,
Boot scootin' boogie.

# Bouquet of Roses

Words and Music by Steve Nelson and Bob Hilliard

recorded by Eddy Arnold, Mickey Gilley


I'm sending you a big bouquet of roses,
One for ev'ry time you broke my heart,
And as the door of love between us closes,
Tears will fall like petals when we part.

I begged you to be diff'rent, but you'll always be untrue.
I'm tired of forgiving, now there's nothing left to do.
So I'm sending you a big bouquet of roses,
One for ev'ry time you broke my heart.

You made our lover's lane a road of sorrow,
Till at last we had to say good-bye.
You're leaving me to face each new tomorrow
With a broken heart you taught to cry.

I know that I should hate you after all you've put me through,
But how can I be bitter when I'm still in love with you?
So I'm sending you a big bouquet of roses,
One for ev'ry time you broke my heart.

# Breathe

Words and Music by Holly Lamar and Stephanie Bentley

recorded by Faith Hill

I can feel the magic floating in the air.
Being with you gets me that way.
I watch the sunlight dance across your face
And I never been this swept away.

All my thoughts just seem to settle on the
    breeze,
When I'm lyin' wrapped up in your arms.
The whole world just fades away,
The only thing I hear is the beating of your
    heart.

*Refrain:*
'Cause I can feel you breathe,
It's washing over me,
And suddenly I'm melting into you.
There's nothing left to prove,
Baby, all we need is just to be
Caught up in the touch,
The slow and steady rush.
Baby, isn't that the way
That love's supposed to be?
I can feel you breathe.
Just breathe.

In a way I know my heart is wakin' up
As all the walls come tumbling down.
Closer than I've ever felt before,
And I know and you know
There's no need for words right now.

*Refrain*

Caught up in the touch,
The slow and steady rush.
Baby, isn't that the way
That love's supposed to be?
I can feel you breathe.
Just breathe.
I can feel the magic floating in the air.
Bein' with you gets me that way.

# A Broken Hearted Me

Words and Music by Randy Goodrum

recorded by Anne Murray

Ev'ry now and then I cry,
Ev'ry night you keep stayin' on my mind.
All my friends say I'll survive,
It just takes time.

*Refrain:*
But I don't think time is gonna heal this broken heart.
No, I don't see how it can if it's broken all apart.
A million miracles could never stop the pain
Or put all the pieces together again.
No, I don't think time is gonna heal this broken heart.
No, I don't see how it can while we are still apart.
And when you hear this song, I hope that you will see
That time won't heal a broken-hearted me.

Ev'ry day is just the same,
Playing games, diff'rent lovers, diff'rent names.
They keep sayin' I'll survive,
It just takes time.

*Refrain*

# Busted

Words and Music by Harlan Howard

recorded by Johnny Cash with The Carter Family, John Conlee


My bills are all due and the baby needs shoes, and I'm busted.
Cotton is down to a quarter a pound, but I'm busted.
I got my cow that went dry and a hen that won't lay,
A big stack of bills that gets bigger each day.
The county's gonna haul my belongings away 'cause I'm busted.

I went to my brother to ask for a loan 'cause I was busted.
I hate to beg like a dog without his bone, but I'm busted.
My brother said, "There ain't a thing I can do.
My wife and my kids are all down with the flu,
And I was just thinking about calling on you, 'cause I'm busted."

Well, I am no thief, but a man can go wrong when he's busted.
The food that we canned that last summer is gone, and I'm busted.
The fields are all bare and the cotton won't grow.
Me and my fam'ly got to pack up and go.
But I'll make a living, just where, I don't know, 'cause I'm busted.

*Spoken:*
I'm broke! No bread! I mean like nothin', forget it!

# By the Time I Get to Phoenix

Words and Music by Jimmy Webb

recorded by Glen Campbell

By the time I get to Phoenix she'll be risin'
She'll find the note I left hangin' on her door.
She'll laugh when she reads the part that says I'm leavin',
'Cause I've left that girl so many times before.

By the time I make Albuquerque she'll be working'
She'll probably stop at lunch and give me a call.
But she'll just hear that phone keep on ringin',
Off the wall.

By the time I make Oklahoma she'll be sleepin'
She'll turn softly and call my name out low.
And she'll cry just to think I'd really leave her,
'Though time and time I've tried to tell her so,
She just didn't know,
I would really go.

# Call Me Mr. In-Between

Words and Music by Harlan Howard

recorded by Burl Ives

Mr. In-Between, Mr. In-Between,
Better leave the scene, Mr. In-Between.

Well, I'm too old for girls and I'm too young
  for women.
I've looked all around and my hopes are
  a-dimmin'.
I feel like a fish not allowed any swimmin',
And it makes a fella mean
To feel he's a part of the lost generation,
A little like a choo-choo that can't find a
  station.
I work like a dog with no recreation.
They call me Mr. In-Between.

Mr. In-Between, Mr. In-Between,
Makes a fellow mean, Mr. In-Between.

Got a hot rod Chevy with the twin carbura-
  tors,
And I know a gal that's a real sharp tomater,
And she's got a daddy with a Caddy that'll
  date 'er.
You see what I mean.
The sweet little thing's just set me a-droolin'.
I'm too big for sodas and I'm too old for
  schoolin',
Too young for lovin' but I'm too old for
  foolin'.
They call me Mr. In-Between.

Mr. In-Between, Mr. In-Between,
Tries to live so clean, Mr. In-Between.

I feel like a sailboat kept in a bottle.
I feel like an engineer that can't find the
  throttle.
I'm too small to walk but I'm too big to
  toddle.
Lawdy, I'm turnin' green
To see all the men makin' time with the
  ladies,
The high school kids at the show with their
  babies,
While I run around like a dog with the
  rabies.
They call me Mr. In-Between.

Mr. In-Between, Mr. In-Between,
Better leave the scene, Mr. In-Between.

# Can't Help Falling in Love

Words and Music by George David Weiss, Hugo Peretti and Luigi Creatore

from the Paramount Picture *Blue Hawaii*
recorded by Elvis Presley, Slim Whitman

Wise men say only fools rush in,
But I can't help falling in love with you.
Shall I stay?
Would it be a sin?
If I can't help falling in love with you.

Like a river flows,
Surely to the sea.
Darling so it goes,
Some things are meant to be.

Take my hand, take my whole life too,
For I can't help falling in love in with you.
For I can't help falling in love with you.

# Candy Kisses

Words and Music by George Morgan

recorded by Elton Britt, Cowboy Copas, Red Foley, Bud Hobbs, Eddie Kirk, George Morgan

Candy kisses wrapped in paper
Mean more to you than any of mine.
Candy kisses wrapped in paper,
You'd rather have them any old time.
You don't mean it when you whisper
Those sweet love words in my ear.
Candy kisses wrapped in paper
Mean more to you than mine do, dear.

I built a castle out of dreams, dear,
I thought that you were building one too.
Now my castles have all fallen,
And I am left alone and blue.
Once my heart was filled with gladness,
Now there's sadness, only tears.
Candy kisses wrapped in paper
Mean more to you than mine do, dear.

# Chains

Words and Music by Bud Reneau and Hal Bynum

recorded by Patty Loveless

Bought a ticket to Seattle, but I can't get to the plane.
Ev'rytime I leave you I keep runnin' out of chain.
My hunger for your lovin' never gives me any slack,
But if I ever break away, I'm never coming back to these

*Refrain:*
Chains, chains, shackles and chains
No matter what it takes, some day I'm gonna break these
Chains, chains, shackles and chains
These love takin', heart breakin', cold, hard, lonely makin' chains

You never try to hold me till you see me walkin' out.
I guess you'd rather be with me than ever be without.
You call me back and kiss me and my heart begins to sink
When I know that all you're doin's takin' up another link in these

*Refrain*

Love was never meant to be a one-way street.
I was never meant to be falling at your feet.
You got me where you want me and I don't know what to do.
You don't belong to me, but I belong to you in these

*Repeat Refrain and Fade*

# The Chair

Words and Music by Hank Cochran and Dean Dillon

recorded by George Strait


Well, excuse me, but I think you've got my chair.
No, that one's not taken; I don't mind if you sit here.
I'll be glad to share.
Yeah, it's usually packed here on Friday nights.
Oh, if you don't mind, could I talk you out of a light.
Well, thank you, could I drink you a buy?
Oh, listen to me. What I mean is, can I buy you a drink?
Anything you please.

Oh, you're welcome. Well, I don't think I caught your name.
Are you waiting for someone to meet you here?
Well, that makes two of us; glad you came.
No, I don't know the name of the band, but they're good, aren't they?
Would you like to dance?
Yeah, I like the song too, it reminds me of you and me, baby.
Do you think there's a chance
That later on I could drive you home?

No, I don't mind at all.
Oh, I like you too, and to tell you the truth
That wasn't my chair after all.
Oh, I like you too, and to tell you the truth
That wasn't my chair after all.

# Charlotte's Web

Words and Music by John Durrill, Cliff Crofford and Snuff Garrett

recorded by The Statler Brothers

Spend the night in Charlotte's bed,
You might get caught in Charlotte's web.
A satin rose that's growin' wild,
Charlotte holds more secrets than the Nile.
She stands and weaves her magic spell.
Her body speaks what words can't tell.
I'm the moth, she's the flame,
In the town that's all too quick to smear her name.

But I'll take the likes of Charlotte and her kind.
Small town talk don't matter now that Charlotte's mine.
It may be true that other men have found her bed.
But I'm the one who's caught in Charlotte's web.

Charlotte took me late one night
To a secret room by candlelight.
She dealt the cards and read my hand
And said she hoped that I would understand.
She turned two cards up face to face.
She said two hearts have found their place.
Now all the rest is history.
The future's full of Charlotte lovin' me.

And I'll take the likes of Charlotte and her kind.
Small town talk don't matter now that Charlotte's mine.
It may be true that other men have found her bed.
But I'm the one who's caught in Charlotte's web.
Charlotte's web.

# Chattahoochee

Words and Music by Jim McBride and Alan Jackson

recorded by Alan Jackson

Way down yonder on the Chattahoochee,
It gets hotter than a hoochie coochie.
We laid rubber on the Georgia asphalt.
Got a little crazy but we never got caught.
Down by the river on a Friday night,
Pyramid of cans in the pale moonlight,
Talking 'bout cars and dreamin' 'bout women.
Never had a plan; just a livin' for the minute.

*Refrain:*
Yeah, way down yonder on the Chattahoochee.
Never knew how much that muddy water meant to me.
But I learned how to swim and I learned who I was;
A lot about livin' and a little 'bout love.

Well, we fogged up the windows in my old Chevy;
I was willin' but she wasn't ready.
So I settled for a burger and a grape sno-cone.
I dropped her off early but I didn't go home.
Down by the river on a Friday night,
Pyramid of cans in the pale moonlight,
Talking 'bout cars and dreamin' 'bout women.
Never had a plan; just a livin' for the minute.

*Refrain*

A lot about livin' and a little 'bout love.

# Chattanoogie Shoe Shine Boy

Words and Music by Harry Stone and Jack Stapp

recorded by Red Foley

Have you ever passed the corner of Fourth and Grand,
Where a little ball of rhythm has a shoe shine stand?
People gather 'round and they clap their hand.
He's a great big bundle of joy.
He pops a boogie woogie rag,
The Chattanoogie shoe shine boy.

He charges you a nickel just to shine one shoe.
He makes the oldest kind of leather look like new.
You feel as though you want to dance when he gets through.
He's a great big bundle of joy.
He pops a boogie woogie rag,
The Chattanoogie shoe shine boy.

It's a wonder that the rag don't tear, the way he makes it pop.
You ought to see him fan the air
With his hoppity-hippity-hippity-hoppity-hoppity-hippity-hop!
He opens up for business when the clock strikes nine.
He likes to get 'em early when they're feelin' fine.
Everybody gets a little rise and shine
With the great big bundle of joy.
He pops a boogie woogie rag,
The Chattanoogie shoe shine boy.

# Chug-A-Lug

Words and Music by Roger Miller

recorded by Roger Miller

Grape wine in a mason jar,
Homemade and brought to school
By a friend of mine after class.
Me and him and this other fool
Decided that we'll drink up what's left,
Chug-a-lug; so we helped ourselves,
First time for ev'rything!
Ummm, my ears still ring.

*Refrain:*
Chug-a-lug, chug-a-lug,
Make you wanta holler hi-de-ho,
Burns your tummy, don'tcha know?
Chug-a-lug, chug-a-lug!

4H and FFA
On a field trip to the farm,
Me and a friend sneak off behind
This big old barn where we uncovered
A covered-up moonshine still,
And we thought we'd drink our fill.
I swallered it with a smile.
I run ten miles.

*Refrain*

Jukebox and a sawdust floor.
Somethin' like I ain't seen before.
And I'm just goin' on fifteen,
But with the help of my faneglin' uncle,
I got snuck in
For my first taste of sin.
I said, "Let me have a big ole sip."
I done a double back flip.

*Refrain*

# Cold, Cold Heart

Words and Music by Hank Williams

recorded by Hank Williams

I tried so hard, my dear, to show
That you're my ev'ry dream.
Yet you're afraid each thing I do
Is just some evil scheme.
A mem'ry from your lonesome past
Keeps us so far apart.
Why can't I free your doubtful mind
And melt your cold, cold heart?

Another love before my time
Made your heart sad and blue,
And so my heart is paying now
For things I didn't do.
In anger, unkind words are said
That make the teardrops start.
Why can't I free your doubtful mind
And melt your cold, cold heart?

You'll never know how much it hurts
To see you sit and cry.
You know you need and want my love,
Yet you're afraid to try.
Why do you run and hide from life?
To try it just ain't smart.
Why can't I free your doubtful mind
And melt your cold, cold heart?

There was a time when I believed
That you belonged to me.
But now I know your heart is shackled
To a memory.
The more I learn to care for you,
The more we drift apart.
Why can't I free your doubtful mind
And melt your cold, cold heart?

# Could I Have This Dance

Words and Music by Wayland Holyfield and Bob House

from the film *Urban Cowboy*
recorded by Anne Murray

I'll always remember
The song they were playing
The first time we danced and I knew.

And we swayed to the music
And held to each other,
I fell in love with you.

*Refrain:*
Could I have this dance for the rest of my life?
Would you be my partner every night?
When we're together it feels so right.
Could I have this dance for the rest of my life?

I'll always remember
That magic moment,
When I held you close to me.
As we moved together,
I knew forever you're all I'll ever need.
You're all I'll ever need.

*Refrain*

# Country Bumpkin

Words and Music by Don Wayne

recorded by Cal Smith

He walked into the bar
And parked his lanky frame upon a tall bar
    stool,
And with a long, soft Southern drawl said,
"I'll have me a glass of anything that's cool."
A barroom girl with hard and knowing eyes
Slowly looked him up and down,
And she thought, "I wonder how on earth
That country bumpkin found his way to
    town."

And she said, "Hello, country bumpkin,
How's the frost out on the pumpkin?
I've seen some sights, but, man, you're
    somethin'.
Where'd you come from, country bumpkin?"

It was just a short year later
In a bed of joy-filled tears yet deathlike pain,
Into this wondrous world of many wonders
One more wonder came.
That same woman's face was wrapped up
In a raptured look of love and tenderness,
As she marveled at the soft and warm
And cuddly boy child feeding at her breast.

And she said, "Hello, country bumpkin,
Fresh as frost out on the pumpkin.
I've seen some sights, but, babe, you're
    somethin'!
Mama loves her country bumpkin."

Forty years of hard work later,
In a simple, quiet, and peaceful country
    place,
The heavy hand of time had not erased
The raptured wonder from the woman's face.
She was lying on her death bed
Knowing fully well her race was nearly run,
But she softly smiled and looked
Into the sad eyes of her husband and her
    son.

*Twice:*
And she said, "So long, country bumpkin,
The frost is gone now from the pumpkin.
I've seen some sights and life's been some-
    thin'.
See you later, country bumpkin."

THE LYRIC LIBRARY

# Cowboy Take Me Away

Words and Music by Martie Seidel and Marcus Hummon

recorded by The Dixie Chicks

I said I wanna touch the earth,
I wanna break it in my hands.
I wanna grow something wild and unruly.
I wanna sleep on the hard ground
In the comfort of your arms
On a pillow of blue bonnets
And a blanket made of stars.
Oh, it sounds good to me. I said,

*Refrain:*
Cowboy, take me away.
Fly this girl as high as you can
Into the wild blue.
Set me free, oh, I pray,
Closer to heaven above
And closer to you, closer to you.

I wanna walk and not run.
I wanna skip and not fall.
I wanna look at the horizon
And not see a building standin' tall.
I wanna be the only one
For miles and miles,
Except for maybe you
And your simple smile.
Oh, it sounds good to me.
Yes, it sounds so good to me.

*Refrain*

I said I wanna touch the earth,
I wanna break it in my hands.
I wanna grow something wild and unruly.
Oh, it sounds so good to me.

*Refrain*

Closer to you.
Cowboy, take me away,
Closer to you.

# Crazy

Words and Music by Willie Nelson

recorded by Patsy Cline and various other artists

Crazy, I'm crazy for feelin' so lonely.
I'm crazy, crazy for feelin' so blue.
I knew you'd love me as long as you wanted,
And then someday you'd leave me for somebody new.

Worry? Why do I let myself worry,
Wonderin' what in the world did I do?

Oh, crazy for thinkin' that my love could hold you.
I'm crazy for tryin' and crazy for cryin'
And I'm crazy for lovin' you!

# Cryin' Time

Words and Music by Buck Owens

recorded by Buck Owens

Now they say that absence makes the heart grow fonder,
And that tears are only rain to make love grow.
Well, my love for you could never grow no stronger
If I lived to be a hundred years old.

*Refrain:*
Oh, it's cryin' time again, you're gonna leave me.
I can see that faraway look in your eyes.
I can tell by the way you hold me, darlin',
That it won't be long before it's cryin' time.

Now you said that you've someone you love better.
That's the way it's happened ev'ry time before.
And as sure as the sun comes up tomorrow,
Cryin' time will start when you walk out the door.

*Refrain*

# Crying in the Chapel

Words and Music by Artie Glenn

recorded by Rex Allen, Darrell Glenn, Elvis Presley


You saw me crying in the chapel,
The tears I shed were tears of joy.
I know the meaning of contentment;
Now I am happy with the Lord.
Just a plain and simple chapel
Where humble people go to pray;
I pray the Lord that I'll grow stronger
As I live from day to day.

I've searched and I've searched but I couldn't find
No way on earth to gain peace of mind.
Now I'm happy in the chapel,
Where people are of one accord.
We gather in the chapel
Just to sing and praise the Lord.

Ev'ry sinner looks for something
That will put his heart at ease;
There is only one true answer,
He must get down on his knees.
Meet your neighbor in the chapel,
Join with him in tears of joy;
You'll know the meaning of contentment,
Then you'll be happy with the Lord.

You'll search and you'll search but you'll never find
No way on earth to gain peace of mind.
Take your troubles to the chapel,
Get down on your knees and pray;
Your burdens will be lighter
And you'll surely find the way.

# D-I-V-O-R-C-E

Words and Music by Bobby Braddock and Curly Putman

recorded by Tammy Wynette

Our little boy is four years old and quite a little man;
So we spell out the words we don't want him to understand,
Like T-O-Y or maybe S-U-R-P-R-I-S-E.
But the words we're hiding from him now tear the heart right out of me.

*Refrain:*
Our D-I-V-O-R-C-E becomes final today;
Me and little J-O-E will be going away.
I love you both, and it will be pure H-E-double-L for me.
Oh, I wish that we could stop this D-I-V-O-R-C-E.

Watch him smile; he thinks it's Christmas or his fifth birthday,
And he thinks C-U-S-T-O-D-Y spells fun or play.
I spell out all the hurtin' words and turn my head when I speak,
Because I can't spell away this hurt that's drippin' down my cheeks.

*Refrain*

# Daddy's Hands

Words and Music by Holly Dunn

recorded by Holly Dunn

I remember Daddy's hands folded silently in prayer
And reaching out to hold me when I had a nightmare.
You could read quite a story in the callouses and lines,
Years of work and worry had left their mark behind.

I remember Daddy's hands, how they held my mama tight,
And patted my back for something done right.
There are things that I've forgotten that I loved about the man,
But I'll always remember the love in Daddy's hands.

*Refrain:*
Daddy's hands were soft and kind when I was crying.
Daddy's hands were hard as steel when I'd done wrong.
Daddy's hands weren't always gentle, but I've come to understand,
There was always love in Daddy's hands.

I remember Daddy's hands, working till they bled,
Sacrificed unselfishly just to keep us all fed.
If I could do things over, I'd live my life again
And never take for granted the love in Daddy's hands.

*Refrain*

# Devoted to You

Words and Music by Boudleaux Bryant

recorded by The Everly Brothers

Darling, you can count on me
Till the sun dries up the sea.
Until then I'll always be
Devoted to you.

I'll be yours through endless time,
I'll adore your charms sublime.
Guess by now you know that I'm
Devoted to you.

I'll never hurt you, I'll never lie,
I'll never be untrue.
I'll never give you reason to cry,
I'd be unhappy if you were blue.

Through the years my love will grow,
Like a river it will flow.
It can't die because I'm so
Devoted to you.

# Diggin' Up Bones

Words and Music by Nat Stuckey, Paul Overstreet and Al Gore

recorded by Randy Travis

Last night I dug your picture out from our old dresser drawer.
I set it on the table and I talked to it till four.
I read some old love letters right up to the break of dawn.
Yeah, I've been sittin' alone, diggin' up bones.

Then I went through the jewelry and I found our wedding rings.
I put mine on my finger and I gave yours a fling
Across this lonely bedroom of our recent broken home.
Yeah, tonight I'm sittin' alone, diggin' up bones.

*Refrain:*
I'm diggin' up bones, I'm diggin' up bones,
Exhuming things that's better left alone.
And I'm resurrecting mem'ries of a love that's dead and gone.
Yeah, tonight I'm sittin' alone, diggin' up bones.

And I went through the closet and I found some things in there,
Like that pretty lingerie that I bought you to wear.
And I recalled how good you looked each time you had it on.
Yeah, tonight I'm sittin' alone, diggin' up bones.

*Refrain*

# Distant Drums

Words and Music by Cindy Walker

recorded by Jim Reeves

I hear the sound of distant drums,
Far away, far away.
And if they call for me to come,
Then I must go, and you must stay.
So, Mary, marry me, let's not wait.
Let's share all the time we can before it's too late.
Love me now, for now is all the time there may be.
If you love me, Mary, Mary, marry me.

I hear the sound of bugles blowing,
Far away, far away.
And if they call, then I must go
Across the sea, so wild and gray.
So, Mary, marry me, let's not wait,
Or the distant drums might change our wedding day.
Love me now, for now is all the time there may be.
If you love me, Mary, Mary, marry me.

# Do You Love as Good as You Look

Words and Music by Charlie Black, Rory Bourke and Jerry Gillespie

recorded by The Bellamy Brothers

Long blonde hair, sky blue eyes,
That well-bred look is easy to recognize.
Tailored dress, fits so fine,
And it adds up to the question on my mind.

*Refrain:*
Honey, do you love as good as you look?
Can you satisfy your man
Like your body says you can?
Judging from the cover,
I'd love to read the book.
Honey, do you love as good as you look?

If you could read my mind,
You might blush blood red,
But then again you might come over here instead.
I see they brought your check,
Now you're bound to go.
If I don't make my move right now I may never know.

*Refrain*

Honey, do you love as good as you look?

# Don't Cheat in Our Home Town

Words and Music by Ray Pennington and Roy Marcum

recorded by Ricky Skaggs


Tonight my heart is beating low and my head is bowed.
You've been seen with my best friend on the other side of town.
I don't mind this waiting, don't mind this runaround,
But if you're gonna cheat on me, don't cheat in our home town.

*Refrain:*
How can I stand up to my friends and look 'em in the eye;
Admit the question that I know would be nothing but lies.
You spend all your past time making me a clown,
So if you're gonna cheat on me, don't cheat in our home town.

Now there are no secrets in this little country town;
Everyone knows everyone for miles and miles around.
Your bright eyes and your sweet smile are driving me insane.
You think it's smart to break my heart and run down my name.

*Refrain*

# Down at the Twist and Shout

Words and Music by Mary Chapin Carpenter

recorded by Mary Chapin Carpenter

*Refrain:*
Saturday night and the moon is out.
I wanna head on over to the Twist and Shout,
Find a two-step partner and a Cajun beat,
When it lifts me up, I'm gonna find my feet
Out in the middle of a big dance floor.
When I hear that fiddle, wanna beg for more.
Wanna dance to a band from a-Louisian'
    tonight.

And I never have wandered down to
    New Orleans,
Never have drifted down a bayou stream.
But I heard that music on the radio,
And I swore some day I was gonna go:
Down Highway 10 past Lafayette,
There's a Baton Rouge, and I won't forget
To send you a card with my regrets,
'Cause I'm never gonna come back home.

*Refrain*

They got a alligator stew and a crawfish pie,
A gulf storm blowin' into town tonight.
Livin' on the delta, it's quite a show.
They got hurricane parties ev'ry time it
    blows.
But here up north it's a cold, cold rain,
And there ain't no cure for my blues today;
Except when the paper says Beausoleil is
    a-comin' into town.
Baby, let's go down.

*Refrain*

Bring your mama, bring your papa, bring
    your sister too.
They got lots of music and lots of room.
When they play you a waltz from a-1910,
You're gonna feel a little bit young again.
Well, you learn to dance with your rock 'n'
    roll,
You learn to swing with do-si-do.
But you learn to love at the fais do do
When you hear a little Jolie Blon.

*Refrain*

# Elvira

Words and Music by Dallas Frazier

Recorded by The Oak Ridge Boys

Elvira, Elvira,
My heart's on fire for Elvira.

Eyes that look like heaven, lips like cherry wine,
That girl can sho' nuff make my little light shine.
I get a funny feeling up and down my spine,
'Cause I know that my Elvira's mine.

*Refrain:*
I'm singin' Elvira, Elvira,
My heart's on fire for Elvira.
Giddy-up, a oom papa oom papa mow mow,
Giddy-up, a oom papa oom papa mow mow,
Hi-yo Silver, away.

Tonight I'm gonna meet her at the Hungry House Cafe,
And I'm gonna give her all the love I can.
She's gonna jump and holler 'cause I saved up my last two dollar
And we're gonna search and find that preacher man.

*Refrain*

# England Swings

Words and Music by Roger Miller

recorded by Roger Miller

*Refrain:*
England swings like a pendulum do,
Bobbies on bicycles two by two.
Westminster Abbey, the tower of Big Ben,
The rosy red cheeks of the little children.

Now if you huff and puff and you fin'lly save enough
Money up to take your family on a trip across the sea.
Take a tip before you take your trip,
Let me tell you where to go: go to England. Oh,

*Refrain*

Mama's old pajamas and your papa's mustache,
Fallin' out the window sill, frolic in the grass,
Tryin' to mock the way they talk, but with all in vain,
Gapin' at the dapper men with derby hats and canes.

*Refrain*

# Faded Love

Words and Music by Bob Wills and Johnny Wills

recorded by Bob Wills, Patsy Cline, Willie Nelson & Ray Price and various other artists

As I look at the letters that you wrote to me,
It's you that I'm thinking of.
As I read the lines that to me were so sweet,
I remember our faded love.

*Refrain:*
I miss you, darling, more and more ev'ry day,
As heaven would miss the stars above.
With ev'ry heartbeat I still think of you
And remember our faded love.

I think of the past and all the pleasures we had
As I watch the mating of the dove.
It was in the springtime that you said good-bye.
I remember our faded love.

*Refrain*

# Faking Love

Words and Music by Bobby Braddock and Matraca Berg

recorded by T.G. Sheppard & Karen Brooks

You turn down the covers, I'll turn down the lights;
As we turn to each other, there's no turning back tonight.
I lay on "I love you," and you lay on your charms,
As we lie here in each other's arms.

*Refrain:*
Faking love, faking love.
Only temporary lovers as we lie here to each other.
We're just faking love.

You put on the coffee, I'll put on a smile;
We'll put each other on and laugh and talk a little while.
There's no use in crying for feeling that's all gone.
We both knew we were lying all along.

*Refrain*

Faking love.
We're just faking love.

# Flowers on the Wall

Words and Music by Lewis Calvin DeWitt

recorded by The Statler Brothers, Eric Heatherly

I've been hearin' you're concerned about my happiness;
But all that thought you're givin' me is conscience, I guess.
If I were walkin' in your shoes, I wouldn't worry none.
While you and your friends are worryin' 'bout me, I'm havin' lots of fun.

*Refrain:*
Countin' flowers on the wall, that don't bother me at all.
Playin' solitaire till dawn with a deck of fifty-one.
Smokin' cigarettes and watchin' "Captain Kangaroo,"
Now don't tell me I've nothin' to do.

Last night I dressed in tails, pretended I was on the town;
As long as I can dream, it's hard to slow this swinger down.
So please don't give a thought to me, I'm really doin' fine,
You can always find me here and havin' quite a time.

*Refrain*

It's good to see you, I must go, I know I look a fright;
Anyway, my eyes are not accustomed to this light.
And my shoes are not accustomed to this hard time street,
So I must go back to my room and make my day complete.

*Refrain*

Don't tell me I've nothin' to do.

# Folsom Prison Blues

Words and Music by John R. Cash

recorded by Johnny Cash

I hear the train a-comin'; it's rollin' 'round the bend.
And I ain't seen the sunshine since I don't know when.
I'm stuck at Folsom Prison, and time keeps draggin' on.
But that train keeps rollin' on down to San Antone.

When I was just a baby, my mama told me, "Son,
Always be a good boy; don't ever play with guns."
But I shot a man in Reno, just to watch him die.
When I hear that whistle blowin', I hang my head and cry.

I bet there's rich folk eatin' in a fancy dining car.
They're prob'ly drinkin' coffee and smokin' big cigars.
But I know I had it comin', I know I can't be free,
But those people keep a-movin', and that's what tortures me.

Well, if they freed me from this prison, if that railroad train was mine,
I bet I'd move on over a little farther down the line.
Far from Folsom Prison, that's where I want to stay,
And I'd let that lonesome whistle blow my blues away.

# For the Good Times

Words and Music by Kris Kristofferson

recorded by Ray Price

Don't look so sad
I know it's over;
But life goes on
And this old world
Will keep on turning.
Let's just be glad
We had some time
To spend together.
There's no need
To watch the bridges
That we're burning.

*Refrain:*
Lay your head
Upon my pillow,
Hold your warm and tender body
Close to mine.
Hear the whisper of the raindrops
Blowing soft against the window
And make believe you love me
One more time
For the good times.

I'll get along;
You'll find another;
And I'll be here
If you should find
You ever need me.
Don't say a word
About tomorrow
Or forever.
There'll be time enough
For sadness
When you leave me.

*Refrain*

# Forever and Ever, Amen

Words and Music by Paul Overstreet and Don Schlitz

recorded by Randy Travis

You may think that I'm talking foolish,
You've heard that I'm wild and I'm free.
You may wonder how I can promise you now
This love that I feel for you always will be.
But you're not just time that I'm killin',
I'm no longer one of those guys.
As sure as I live, this love that I give
Is gonna be yours until the day that I die.

Oh, baby, I'm gonna love you forever,
Forever and ever, amen.
As long as old men sit and talk about the
    weather,
As long as old women sit and talk about old
    men;
If you wonder how long I'll be faithful,
I'll be happy to tell you again.
I'm gonna love you forever and ever,
Forever and ever, amen.

They say time take its toll on a body,
Makes a young girl's brown hair turn gray.
Well, honey, I don't care, I ain't in love with
    your hair,
And if it all fell out, well, I'd love you anyway.
They say time can play tricks on a mem'ry,
Make people forget things they knew.
Well, it's easy to see it's happenin' to me.
I've already forgotten ev'ry woman but you.

Oh, darlin', I'm gonna love you forever,
Forever and ever, amen.
As long as old men sit and talk about the
    weather,
As long as old women sit and talk about old
    men,
If you wonder how long I'll be faithful,
Well, just listen to how this song ends.
I'm gonna love you forever and ever,
Forever and ever, amen.
I'm gonna love you forever and ever,
Forever and ever, forever and ever,
Forever and ever, amen.

# Four Walls

Words and Music by Marvin J. Moore and George H. Campbell, Jr.

recorded by Jim Reeves

Out where the bright lights are glowing,
You're drawn like a moth to a flame.
You laugh while the wine's overflowing,
While I sit and whisper your name.

*Refrain:*
Four walls to hear me,
Four walls to see,
Four walls too near me,
Closing in on me.

Sometimes I ask why I'm waiting,
But my walls have nothing to say.
I'm made for love, not for hating,
So here, where you left me, I'll stay.

*Refrain*

One night with you is like heaven,
And so while I'm walking the floor,
I'll listen for steps in the hallway
And wait for your knock on my door.

*Refrain*

Closing in on me.

# Friends in Low Places

Words and Music by Dewayne Blackwell and Earl Bud Lee

recorded by Garth Brooks

Blame it all on my roots.
I showed up in boots
And ruined your black-tie affair.
The last one to know;
The last one to show;
I was the last one you thought you'd
   see there.

And I saw the surprise
And the fear in his eyes
When I took his glass of champagne
And I toasted you,
Said, "Honey, we may be through
But you'll never hear me complain."

*Refrain:*
'Cause I've got friends in low places
Where whiskey drowns
And the beer chases blues away.
And I'll be okay.
Yeah, I'm not big on social graces.
Think I'll slip on down to the oasis.
Oh, I've got friends in low places.

Well, I guess I was wrong.
I just don't belong,
But then I've been there before.
Ev'rything's alright.
I'll just say goodnight
And I'll show myself to the door.

Hey, I didn't mean
To cause a big scene
Just give me an hour and then,
Well I'll be as high
As that ivory tower
That you're livin' in.

*Refrain Twice*

# From Graceland to the Promised Land

Words and Music by Merle Haggard

recorded by Merle Haggard

From the Sun years of the Fifties and the birth of rock and roll,
Millions screamed to see him do his thing.
Elvis touched the life of ev'ry ear that heard him,
And they couldn't help but listen when he sang.

*Refrain:*
It's a long way from Memphis to that mansion in the sky,
But he kept his faith in Jesus all along.
It's a long way from Graceland across Jordan to the Promised Land,
But Jesus fin'lly came to lead him home.

From the days of "Love Me Tender" to his mama's last farewell,
Some say he knew how long he had to stay.
His life was two days longer than the one who gave him life,
And he almost knew the number of the days.

*Refrain*

# Funny How Time Slips Away

Words and Music by Willie Nelson

recorded by Narvel Felts, Billy Walker and various other artists


Well, hello there,
My, it's been a long, long time.
How'm I doin'?
Oh, I guess that I'm doin' fine.
It's been so long now,
Yet it seems like it was only yesterday.
Ain't it funny how time slips away.

How's your new love?
I hope that he's doin' fine.
Heard you told him
That you'd love him till the end of time.
Now, that's the same thing
That you told me, seems like only yesterday.
Ain't it funny how time slips away.

Gotta go now,
Guess I'll see you around.
Don't know when, though,
Never know when I'll be back in town.
Just remember what I told you,
That in time you're gonna pay.
And it's surprising how time slips away.

# Funny Way of Laughin'

Words and Music by Hank Cochran

recorded by Burl Ives

If you see me with a great big smile
At some party where the fun runs wild,
If tears start to flow and I fall apart,
Please don't think you broke my heart.

*Refrain:*
It's just my funny way of laughin',
Yes, my funny way of laughin'.
Your leavin' didn't bother me.
It's just my funny way of laughin',
Yes, my funny way of laughin'.
I'm really happy as can be.

If we meet on the street
And a little bitty tear rolls down my cheek,
Please don't think it's because I'm blue
Or that I'm still in love with you.

*Refrain*

Remember the day you left our place
And how the tears rolled down my face.
It wasn't because you were leaving me;
I was happy because you were pleasing me.

*Refrain*

# The Gambler

Words and Music by Don Schlitz

recorded by Kenny Rogers

On a warm summer's evenin'
On a train bound for nowhere,
I met up with the gambler.
We were both too tired to sleep.
So we took turns a starin'
Out the window at the darkness
'Til boredom overtook us,
And he began to speak.
He said, "Son, I've made a life
Out of readin' people's faces,
And knowin' what their cards were,
By the way they held their eyes.
And if you don't mind my sayin',
I can see you're out of aces.
For a taste of your whiskey
I'll give you some advice."

So I handed him my bottle
And he drank down my last swallow.
Then he bummed a cigarette,
And he asked me for a light.
And the night got deathly quiet,
And his face lost all expression.
Said, "If you're gonna play the game, boy,
Ya gotta learn to play it right.

*Refrain:*
You got to know when to hold 'em,
Know when to fold 'em,
Know when to walk away,
And know when to run.
You never count your money
When you're sittin' at the table,
There'll be time enough for countin'
When the dealin's done.

Every gambler knows
That the secret to survivin'
Is knowin' what to throw away
And knowin' what to keep.
'Cause every hand's a winner
And every hand's a loser,
And the best that you can hope for
Is to die in your sleep."
And when he'd finished speakin',
He turned back towards the window,
Crushed out his cigarette,
And faded off to sleep.
And somewhere in the darkness,
The gambler, he broke even.
But in his final words,
I found an ace that I could keep.

*Refrain Twice*

# Gentle on My Mind

Words and Music by John Hartford

recorded by Glen Campbell

It's knowing that your door is always open,
And your path is free to walk,
That makes me tend to leave my sleeping bag
Rolled up and stashed behind your couch.
And it's knowing I'm not shackled by forgotten words and bonds
And the ink stains that are dried upon some line
That keeps you in the backroads by the rivers of my memory,
That keeps you ever gentle on my mind.

It's not clinging to the rocks and ivy
Planted on their columns now that bind me
Or something that somebody said
Because they thought we fit together walkin'.
It's just knowing that the world will not be cursing or forgiving
When I walk along some railroad track and find
That you're moving on the backroads by the rivers of my memory
And for hours you're just gentle on my mind.

Though the wheat fields and the clothes lines
And the junkyards and the highways come between us,
And some other woman's cyring to her mother
'Cause she turned and I was gone.
I still might run in silence, tears of joy might stain my face,
And a summer sun might burn me 'til I'm blind,
But not to where I cannot see you walkin' on the backroads
By the rivers flowing gentle on my mind.

I dip my cup of soup back
From a gurglin', cracklin' cauldron in some train yard,
My beard a rough'nin' coal pile
And a dirty hat pulled low across my face.
Through cupped hands 'round the tin can
I pretend I hold you to my breast, and find
That you're waving from the backroads by the rivers of my mem'ries
Ever smilin', ever gentle on my mind.

# A Girl's Night Out

Words and Music by Brent Maher and Jeff Hawthorne Bullock

recorded by The Judds

Friday fin'lly came around.
This girl's ready to paint the town.
Tonight ain't nothing gonna slow me down.
I did my time working all week.
Tonight's all mine. Tomorrow I'll sleep.
I wanna hear a band with a country sound.
I've been cooped up all week long.
I've been working my fingers to the bone.

*Refrain:*
Well, it's a girl's night out.
Honey, there ain't no doubt.
I'm gonna dance ev'ry dance till the boys go home.
Well, it's my night to rock.
No watching that old clock.
Oh, ain't no doubt, Lawdy, it's a girl's night out.

Two-step or the cotton-eyed joe,
They can play 'em fast or they can play 'em slow.
I can do 'em all, just show me the floor.
You can give me a little rock and roll,
Or even a waltz with the lights down low.
I'll still be dancing when they close the doors.
I've been cooped up all week long.
I've been working my fingers to the bone.

*Refrain Twice*

# Gone

Words and Music by Smokey Rogers

recorded by Ferlin Husky

Since you've gone,
The moon, the sun, the stars in the sky
Know the reason why I cry.
Love divine once was mine;
Now you've gone.

Since you've gone,
My heart, my lips, my tear-dimmed eyes,
A lonely soul within me cries.
I acted smart, broke your heart;
Now you've gone.

Oh, what I'd give
For the lifetime I've wasted,
The love that I've tasted.
I was wrong; now you've gone.

# A Good Hearted Woman

Words and Music by Willie Nelson and Waylon Jennings

recorded by Waylon Jennings & Willie Nelson

A long time forgotten
Are dreams that just fell by the way.
And the good life he promised
Ain't what she's living today.
But she never complains
Of the bad times or bad things he's done, Lord.
She just talks about the good times they've had
And all the good times to come.

*Refrain:*
She's a good-hearted woman
In love with a good-timin' man.
She loves him in spite of his ways
That she don't understand.
Through teardrops and laughter,
They'll pass through this world hand in hand,
A good-hearted woman
Lovin' her good-timin' man.

He likes the night life,
The bright lights, and good-timin' friends.
When the party's all over,
She'll welcome him back home again.
Lord knows she don't understand him,
But she does the best that she can.
'Cause she's a good-hearted woman;
She loves her good-timin' man.

*Refrain*

# Grandpa (Tell Me 'bout the Good Old Days)

Words and Music by Jamie O'Hara

recorded by The Judds

Grandpa, tell me 'bout the good old days.
Sometimes it feels like this world's gone crazy.
Grandpa, take me back to yesterday
When the line between right and wrong didn't seem so hazy.

*Refrain:*
Did lovers really fall in love to stay,
And stand beside each other, come what may?
Was a promise really something people kept,
Not just something they would say (and then forget)?
Did fam'lies really bow their heads to pray?
Did daddies really never go away?
Oh, oh, Grandpa, tell me 'bout the good old days.

Grandpa, ev'rything is changin' fast.
We call it progress, but I just don't know.
And Grandpa, let's wander back into the past,
Then paint me the picture of long ago.

*Refrain*

Oh, oh, grandpa, tell me 'bout the good old days.

# Green Green Grass of Home

Words and Music by Curly Putman

recorded by Porter Wagoner

It's good to touch the green, green grass of home.

The old home town looks the same
As I step down from the train,
And there to meet me is my mama and papa.
Down the road I look and there runs Mary,
Hair of gold and lips like cherries.
Its good to touch the green, green grass of home.

*Refrain:*
Yes, they'll all come to meet me,
Arms reaching, smiling sweetly;
It's good to touch the green, green grass of home.

The old house is still standing
Tho' the paint is cracked and dry,
And there's that old oak tree that I used to play on.

Down the lane I walk with my sweet Mary,
Hair of gold and lips like cherries.
It's good to touch the green, green grass of home.

*Refrain*

*Spoken:*
Then I awake and look around me
At four gray walls that surround me
And I realize that I was only dreaming.

For there's a guard and there's a sad old padre,
Arm in arm we'll walk at daybreak.
Again I'll touch the green, green grass of home.

Yes, they'll all come to see me,
In the shade of that old oak tree
As they lay me 'neath the green, green grass of home.

# Half as Much

Words and Music by Curley Williams

recorded by Hank Williams and various other artists

If you loved me half as much as I love you,
You wouldn't worry me half as much as you do.
You're nice to me when there's no one else around.
You only build me up to let me down.

If you missed me half as much as I miss you,
You wouldn't stay away half as much as you do.
I know that I would never be this blue,
If you only loved me half as much as I love you.

# The Happiest Girl in the Whole U.S.A.

Words and Music by Donna Fargo

recorded by Donna Fargo

Good morning, morning. Hello, sunshine.
Wake up, sleepy head.
Why'd we move that beau-jungle clock
So far away from the bed?
Just one more minute, that's why we moved it,
One more hug or two.
Do you love wakin' up next to me
As much as I love wakin' up next to you?

You make the coffee, I'll make the bed.
I'll fix your lunch and you fix mine.
Now tell me the truth,
Do these old shoes look funny?
Honey, it's almost time.
Now you be careful, gotta go.
I love you, have a beautiful day,
And kiss the happiest girl in the whole U.S.A.

Skip-a-dee-doo-dah, thank you, Lord,
For making him for me.
And thank you for letting life turn out the way
That I always thought it could be.
There once was a time when I could not imagine
How it would feel to say,
I'm the happiest girl in the whole U.S.A.

*Repeat and Fade:*
Now shine on me, sunshine,
Walk with me, world.
It's a skip-a-dee-doo-dah day,
And I'm the happiest girl in the whole U.S.A.

# Harper Valley P.T.A.

Words and Music by Tom T. Hall

recorded by Jeannie C. Riley

I want to tell you all a story
'Bout a Harper Valley widowed wife
Who had a teenage daughter
Who attended Harper Valley Junior High.
Well her daughter came home one
   afternoon,
And didn't even stop to play;
She said, "Mom I got a note here
From the Harper Valley P.T.A."

The note said, "Misses Johnson
You're wearing your dresses way too high;
It's reported you've been drinking
And a-runnin' 'round with men and
   goin' wild:
And we don't believe you ought to be
A-bringing up your little girl this way."
It was signed by the secretary.
Harper Valley P.T.A.

Well, it happened that the P.T.A.
Was gonna meet that very afternoon;
They were sure surprised when
   Misses Johnson
Wore her mini-skirt into the room.
And as she walked up to the blackboard,
I still recall the words she had to say;
She said, "I'd like to address this meeting
Of the Harper Valley P.T.A."

Well there's Bobby Taylor sittin' there,
And seven times he's asked me for a date;
Misses Taylor sure seems to use a lot of ice
Whenever he's away.

And Mister Baker, can you tell us
Why your secretary had to leave this town,
And shouldn't Widow Jones be told
To keep her window shades all pulled
   completely down?"

Well Mister Harper couldn't be here
'Cause he stayed too long at Kelly's bar again,
And if you smell Shirley Thompson's breath,
You'll find she's had a little nip of gin.

Then you have the nerve to tell me
You think that as a mother I'm not fit,
Well, this is just a little Peyton Place,
And you're all Harper Valley hypocrites."

No I wouldn't put you on because it
   really did,
It happened just this way,
The day my Mama socked it to
The Harper Valley P.T.A.
The day my Mama socked it to
The Harper Valley P.T.A.

# He Stopped Loving Her Today

Words and Music by Bobby Braddock and Curly Putman

recorded by George Jones

He said, "I'll love you 'til I die."
She told him, "You'll forget in time."
As the years went slowly by,
She still preyed upon his mind.

He kept her picture on his wall,
Went half crazy now and then;
But he still loved her through it all,
Hoping she'd come back again.

He kept some letters by his bed,
Dated 1962.
He had underlined in red
Every single "I love you."

I went to see him just today,
Oh, but I didn't see no tears.
All dressed up to go away,
First time I'd seen him smile in years.

*Refrain:*
He stopped loving her today.
They placed a wreath upon his door,
And soon they'll carry him away.
He stopped loving her today.

*Spoken:*
You know, she came to see him one last time.
We all wondered if she would.
And it came running through my mind,
This time he's over her for good.

*Refrain*

# He Thinks He'll Keep Her

Words and Music by Mary Chapin Carpenter and Don Schlitz

recorded by Mary Chapin Carpenter

She makes his coffee, she makes his bed,
She does the laundry, she keeps him fed.
When she was twenty-one, she wore her mother's lace,
She said forever with a smile upon her face.

She does the carpool, she P.T.A.'s,
Doctors and dentists, she drives all day.
When she was twenty-nine she delivered number three,
And every Christmas card showed a perfect family.

*Refrain:*
Everything runs right on time, years of practice and design.
Spit and polish 'til it shines, he thinks he'll keep her.
Everything is so benign, the safest place you'll ever find,
God forbid you'd change your mind, he thinks he'll keep her.

She packs his suitcase, she sits and waits,
With no expression upon her face.
When she was thirty-six she met him at their door,
She said, "I'm sorry, I don't love you anymore."

*Refrain*

For fifteen years she had a job and not one raise in pay,
Now she's in the typing pool at minimum wage.

Everything runs right on time, years of practice and design.
Spit and polish 'til it shines, he thinks he'll keep her.
Everything is so benign, the safest place you'll ever find,
At least until you change your mind.
He thinks he'll keep her.

# He'll Have to Go

Words and Music by Joe Allison and Audrey Allison

recorded by Jim Reeves

Put your sweet lips a little closer to the phone.
Let's pretend that we're together all alone.
I'll tell the man to turn the jukebox way down low.
And you can tell your friend there with you he'll have to go.

Whisper to me, tell me do you love me true,
Or is he holding you the way I do?
Though love is blind, make up your mind, I've got to know.
Should I hang up or will you tell him he'll have to go?

You can't say the words I want to hear
While you're with another man.
If you want me, answer "yes" or "no,"
Darling, I will understand.

*Repeat Verse 1*

# Heartaches by the Number

Words and Music by Harlan Howard

recorded by Ray Price and various other artists

Heartache number one was when you left me,
I never knew that I could hurt this way.
And heartache number two was when you came back again,
You came back and never meant to stay.

*Refrain:*
Now I've got heartaches by the number, troubles by the score.
Ev'ry day you love me less, each day I love you more.
Yes, I've got heartaches by the number, a love that I can't win,
But the day that I stop counting, that's the day my world will end.

Heartache number three was when you called me
And said that you were coming back to stay.
With hopeful heart I waited for your knock on the door,
I waited, but you must have lost your way.

*Refrain*

# Hello Walls

Words and Music by Willie Nelson

recorded by Faron Young

Hello, walls,
How'd things go for you today?
Don't you miss her
Since she up and walked away?
And I'll bet you dread to spend
Another lonely night with me,
But, lonely walls, I'll keep you company.

Hello, window,
Well, I see that you're still here.
Aren't you lonely
Since our darlin' disappeared?
Well, look here, is that a teardrop
In the corner of your pane?
Now, don't you try to tell me that it's rain.

She went away and left us all alone,
The way she planned.
Guess we'll have to learn to get along
Without her if we can.

Hello, ceiling,
I'm gonna stare at you awhile.
You know I can't sleep,
So won't you bear with me awhile?
We must all pull together
Or else I'll lose my mind,
'Cause I've got a feelin'
She'll be gone a long, long time.

# Help Me Make It Through the Night

Words and Music by Kris Kristofferson

recorded by Sammi Smith, Willie Nelson

Take the ribbon from your hair,
Shake it loose and let it fall,
Layin' soft against my skin
Like the shadows on the wall.

Come and lay down by my side
Till the early mornin' light.
All I'm takin' is your time.
Help me make it through the night.

I don't care who's right or wrong,
I don't try to understand.
Let the devil take tomorrow.
Lord, tonight I need a friend.

Yesterday is dead and gone
And tomorrow's out of sight.
And it's sad to be alone.
Help me make it through the night.

# Here Comes My Baby

Words and Music by Dottie West and Bill West

recorded by Dottie West

Here comes more tears to cry;
Here comes more heartaches by;
Here comes my baby back again.
Here comes more misery;
Here comes old memories;
Here comes my baby back again!

My arms are open wide
To let more hurt inside;
Here comes my baby back again.
He's sorry once again;
Once more I'll understand.
Here comes my baby back again.
Here comes my baby back again.

# Here You Come Again

Words by Cynthia Weil
Music by Barry Mann

recorded by Dolly Parton

Here you come again,
Just when I've begun to get myself together.
You waltz right in the door,
Just like you've done before,
And wrap my heart 'round your little finger.

Here you come again,
Just when I'm about to make it work without you.
You look into my eyes,
And lie those pretty lies,
And pretty soon I'm wond'rin' how I came to doubt you.

*Refrain:*
All you gotta do is smile that smile
And there go all my defenses.
Just leave it up to you and in a little while
You're messin' up my mind and fillin' up my senses.

Here you come again,
Lookin' better than a body has a right to,
And shakin' me up so that all I really know
Is here you come again,
And here I go.

*Refrain*

Here you come again,
Lookin' better than a body has a right to,
And shakin' me up so that all I really know
Is here you come again,
And here I go.
Here I go.

# Here's a Quarter (Call Someone Who Cares)

Words and Music by Travis Tritt

recorded by Travis Tritt

You say you were wrong to ever leave me alone,
And now you're sorry. You're lonesome and scared.
And you say you'd be happy if you could just come back home.
Well, here's a quarter. Call someone who cares.

*Refrain:*
Call someone who'll listen and might give a damn.
Maybe one of your sordid affairs.
But don't you come around here handing me none of your lines.
Here's a quarter. Call someone who cares.

Girl, I thought what we had could never turn bad,
So your leaving caught me unaware.
But the fact is you've run. Girl, that can't be undone.
So, here's a quarter. Call someone who cares.

*Refrain*

Yeah, here's a quarter. Call someone who cares.
Yeah, yeah.

# Hey, Good Lookin'

Words and Music by Hank Williams

recorded by Hank Williams

*Refrain:*
Hey, hey, good loookin'
Whatcha got cookin'
How's about cookin' somethin' up with me?

Hey, sweet baby,
Don't you think maybe
We could find us a brand new recipe?

I got a hot rod and a Ford and a two dollar bill
And I know a spot right over the hill.
There's soda pop and the dancin's free,
So if you wanna have fun come along with me.

*Refrain*

I'm free and ready
So we can go steady.
How's about savin' all your time for me.

No more lookin'
I know I've been tooken.
How's about keepin' steady company?

I'm gonna throw my date book over the fence
And find me one for five or ten cents;
I'll keep it 'til it's covered with age
'Cause I'm writin' your name down on every page.

*Refrain*

# Honky Tonk Blues

Words and Music by Hank Williams

recorded by Hank Williams, Charley Pride

I left my home down on a rural route
And told my folks I'm goin' steppin' out
To get the honky tonk blues,
The jumpin' honky tonk blues.
Lord, I got 'em, I got the honky tonk blues.

I went to a dance, wore out my shoes,
Woke up this mornin' wishin' I could lose
The jumpin' honky tonk blues,
The weary honky tonk blues.
Lord, I'm sufferin' with the honky tonk blues.

I stepped into ev'ry place in town.
This city life has really got me down.
I got the honky tonk blues.
I got the honky tonk blues.
Lord, I'm sufferin' with the honky tonk blues.

When I get home again to Ma and Pa,
I know they're gonna lay down the law
About the honky tonk blues,
The jumpin' honky tonk blues.
Lord, I'm sufferin' with the honky tonk blues.

Gonna tuck my worries underneath my arm
And get right back to my pappy's farm,
And leave the honky tonk blues.
Forget the honky tonk blues.
I don't want to be bothered with the honky tonk blues.

# Honky Tonkin'

Words and Music by Hank Williams

recorded by Hank Williams; Hank Williams Jr.

When you are sad and lonely
And have no place to go,
Just come to see me, baby,
And bring along some dough.

*Refrain:*
And we'll go honky tonkin', honky tonkin'.
Honky tonkin', honey baby,
We'll go honky tonkin' 'round this town.

When you and your baby
Have a fallin' out,
Just call me up, sweet mama,
And we'll go steppin' out.

*Refrain*

We're goin' into the city,
To the city fair.
If you go to the city,
You will find me there.

*Refrain*

# Husbands and Wives

Words and Music by Roger Miller

recorded by Roger Miller, Brooks & Dunn

Two broken hearts, lonely,
Lookin' like houses where nobody lives.
Two people, each havin' so much pride inside,
Neither side forgives.
The angry words spoken in haste,
Such a waste of two lives.
It's my belief pride is the chief cause
In the decline in the number of husbands and wives.

A woman and a man, a man and a woman,
Some can, some can't, and some can't.

*Repeat Verse 1*

Yeah, it's my belief pride is the chief cause
In the decline in the number of husbands and wives.

# I Almost Lost My Mind

Words and Music by Ivory Joe Hunter

recorded by Ivory Joe Hunter

When I lost my baby,
I almost lost my mind.
When I lost my baby,
I almost lost my mind.
My head is in a spin
Since she left me behind.

I pass a million people,
I can't tell who I meet.
I pass a million people,
I can't tell who I meet,
'Cause my eyes are full of tears.
Where can my baby be?

I went to see a gypsy
And had my fortune read.
I went to see a gypsy
And had my fortune read.
I hung my head in sorrow
When she said what she said.

I can tell you, people,
The news was not so good.
Well, I can tell you, people,
The news was not so good.
She said, "Your baby has quit you.
This time she's gone for good."

# I Believe the South Is Gonna Rise Again

Words and Music by Bobby Braddock

recorded by Tanya Tucker

Mama never had a flower garden,
'Cause cotton grew right up to our front door.
And Daddy never went on a vacation;
He died a tired old man of forty-four.
Our neighbors in the big house called us "redneck,"
'Cause we lived in a poor sharecropper shack.
The Jacksons down the road were poor like we were,
But our skin was white and theirs was black.

But I believe the South is gonna rise again,
But not the way we thought it would back then.
I mean ev'rybody hand in hand.
I believe the South is gonna rise again.

I see wooded parks and big skyscrapers
Where once stood red clay hills and cotton fields.
I see sons and daughters of sharecroppers
Drinking scotch and making business deals.
But more important, I see human progress,
As we forget the bad and keep the good.
A brand new breeze is blowin' 'cross the southland,
And I see a brand new kind of brotherhood.

Yes, I believe the South is gonna rise again,
But not the way we thought it would back then.
I mean ev'rybody hand in hand.
I believe the South is gonna rise again.

# I Can Love You Like That

Words and Music by Maribeth Derry, Jennifer Kimball and Steve Diamond

recorded by John Michael Montgomery

They read you Cinderella, you hoped it
    would come true
That one day your Prince Charming would
    come rescue you.
You like romantic movies; you never will
    forget
The way you felt when Romeo kissed Juliet.
All this time that you've been waiting,
You don't have to wait no more.

*Refrain:*
I can love you like that.
I would make you my world,
Move heaven and earth if you were my girl.
I will give you my heart, be all that you need,
Show you you're ev'rything that's precious
    to me.
If you give me a chance, I can love you like
    that.

I never make a promise that I don't intend
    to keep.
So when I say forever, forever's what I mean.
I'm no Casanova, but I swear this much is
    true:
I'll be holding nothing back when it comes
    to you.
You dream of love that's everlasting.
Well, baby, open up your eyes.

*Refrain*

You want tenderness, I got tenderness.
And I see through to the heart of you.
If you want a man who understands,
You don't have to look very far.
I can love you, I can,

*Repeat and Fade:*
I can love you like that.
I would make you my world,
Move heaven and earth if you were my girl.
I will give you my heart, be all that you need,
Show you you're ev'rything that's precious
    to me.

# I Can't Help It (If I'm Still in Love with You)

Words and Music by Hank Williams

recorded by Hank Williams, Linda Ronstadt

*Refrain:*
Today I passed you on the street,
And my heart fell at your feet.
I can't help it if I'm still in love with you.
Somebody else stood by your side,
And he looked so satisfied.
I can't help it if I'm still in love with you.

A picture from the past came slowly stealing
As I brushed your arm and walked so close to you.
Then suddenly I got that old-time feeling.
I can't help it if I'm still in love with you.

*Refrain*

It's hard to know another's lips will kiss you
And hold you just the way I used to do.
Oh, heaven only knows how much I miss you.
I can't help it if I'm still in love with you.

# I Can't Stop Loving You

Words and Music by Don Gibson

recorded by Conway Twitty, Kitty Wells, Don Gibson, and various other artists

Those happy hours that we once knew,
Though long ago, still make me blue.
They say that time heals a broken heart,
But time has stood still since we've been apart.

I can't stop loving you, so I've made up my mind
To live in memory of old lonesome times.
I can't stop wanting you, it's useless to say,
So I'll just live my life in dreams of yesterday.

*Repeat Verse 1*

I can't stop loving you, there's no use to try.
Pretend there's someone new; I can't live a lie.
I can't stop wanting you the way that I do.
There's only been one love for me, that one love is you.

# I Fall to Pieces

Words and Music by Hank Cochran and Harlan Howard

recorded by Patsy Cline and various other artists

I fall to pieces
Each time I see you again.
I fall to pieces.
How can I be just your friend?
You want me to act like we've never kissed.
You want me to forget,
Pretend we've never met,
And I've tried and I've tried,
But I haven't yet.
You walk by,
And I fall to pieces.

I fall to pieces
Each time someone speaks your name.
I fall to pieces.
Time only adds to the flame.
You tell me to find someone else to love.
Someone who'll love me, too,
The way you used to do,
But each time I go out with someone new,
You walk by,
And I fall to pieces.
You walk by,
And I fall to pieces.

# I Feel Lucky

Words and Music by Mary Chapin Carpenter and Don Schlitz

recorded by Mary Chapin Carpenter


Well, I woke up this morning, stumbled out of my rack.
I opened up the paper to the page in the back.
It only took a minute for my finger to find
My daily dose of destiny under my sign.
My eyes just about popped out of my head.
It said, "The stars are stacked against you, girl. Get back in bed."

I feel lucky, I feel lucky, yeah.
No Professor Doom gonna stand in my way.
Mm, I feel lucky today.

Well, I strolled down to the corner, gave my numbers to the clerk.
The pot's eleven million, so I called in sick to work.
I bought a pack of Camels, a burrito, and a Barq's,
Crossed against the light, made a beeline for the park.
The sky began to thunder, the wind began to moan.
I heard a voice above me sayin', "Girl, you better get back home."

I feel lucky, I feel lucky, yeah.
No tropical depression gonna steal my sun away.
Mm, I feel lucky today.

Now eleven million later, I was sittin' at the bar.
I'd bought the house a double, then the waitress a new car.
Dwight Yoakam's in the corner, try'n' to catch my eye.
Lyle Lovett's right beside me with his hand upon my thigh.
The moral of this story, it's simple but it's true:
Hey, the stars might lie, but the numbers never do.

I feel lucky, I feel lucky, yeah.
Hey Dwight, hey Lyle, boys, you don't have to fight.
Hot dog, I'm feeling lucky tonight.

I feel lucky, I feel lucky, yeah.
Think I'll flip a coin, I'm a winner either way.
Mm, I feel lucky today.

# I Hope You Dance

Words and Music by Tia Sillers and Mark D. Sanders

recorded by Lee Ann Womack with Sons of the Desert

I hope you never lose your sense of wonder,
You get your fill to eat, but always keep that hunger.
May you never take one single breath for granted.
God forbid love ever leave you empty handed.
I hope you still feel small when you stand beside the ocean.
Whenever one door closes, I hope one more opens.
Promise me that you'll give faith a fighting chance.
And when you get the choice to sit it out or dance,
I hope you dance. I hope you dance.

I hope you never fear those mountains in the distance,
Never settle for the path of least resistance.
Livin' might mean takin' chances if they're worth takin'.
Lovin' might be a mistake, but it's worth makin'.
Don't let some hell-bent heart leave you bitter.
When you come close to sellin' out, reconsider.
Give the heavens above more than just a passing glance.
And when you get the choice to sit it out or dance,
I hope you dance. I hope you dance.

(Time is a wheel in constant motion, always rolling us along.
Tell me, who wants to look back on their youth
And wonder where those years have gone?)

I hope you still feel small when you stand beside the ocean.
Whenever one door closes, I hope one more opens.
Promise me that you'll give faith a fighting chance.
And when you get the choice to sit it out or dance,
Dance. I hope you dance.

(Time is a wheel in constant motion, always rolling us along.
Tell me, who wants to look back on their youth
And wonder where those years have gone?)

# I Just Fall in Love Again

Words and Music by Larry Herbstritt, Stephen H. Dorff, Gloria Sklerov and Harry Lloyd

recorded by Anne Murray

Dreamin', I must be dreamin';
Or am I really lyin' here with you?
Baby, you take me in your arms,
And though I'm wide awake
I know my dream is comin' true.

*Refrain:*
And, oh, I just fall in love again;
Just one touch and then it happens ev'ry time.
And there I go, I just fall in love again,
And when I do, I can't help myself,
I fall in love with you.

Magic, it must be magic,
The way I hold you and the night just seems to fly.
Easy for you to take me to a star.
Heaven is that moment when I look into your eyes.

*Refrain*

Can't help myself, I fall in love with you.

# ('Til) I Kissed You

Words and Music by Don Everly

recorded by The Everly Brothers

Never felt like this until I kissed you.
How did I exist until I kissed you?
Never had you on my mind;
Now you're there all the time.
Never knew what I missed until I kissed you.
Uh-huh, I kissed you, oh yeah.

Things have really changed since I kissed you.
My life's not the same now that I kissed you.
Mmm, you got a way about you;
Now I can't live without you.
Never knew what I missed until I kissed you.
Uh-huh, I kissed you, oh yeah.

You don't realize what you do to me.
And I didn't realize what a kiss could be.
Mmm, you got a way about you;
Now I can't live without you.
Never knew what I missed until I kissed you.
Uh-huh, I kissed you,
Oh yeah, I kissed you.

# I Love a Rainy Night

Words and Music by Eddie Rabbitt, Even Stevens and David Malloy

recorded by Eddie Rabbitt


Well, I love a rainy night;
I love a rainy night.
I love to hear the thunder, watch the lightning
When it lights up the sky,
You know it makes me feel good.
Well, I love a rainy night;
It's such a beautiful sight.
I love to feel the rain on my face,
Taste the rain on my lips
In the moonlight shadows.
Showers wash all my cares away;
I wake up to a sunny day.

*Refrain:*
'Cause I love a rainy night,
Yeah, I love a rainy night.
Well, I love a rainy night.
Well, I love a rainy night.

Well, I love a rainy night;
I love a rainy night.
I love to hear the thunder, watch the lightning
When it lights up the sky,
You know it makes me feel good.
Well, I love a rainy night;
It's such a beautiful sight.
I love to feel the rain on my face,
Taste the rain on my lips
In the moonlight shadows.
Puts a song in this heart of mine;
Puts a smile on my face ev'ry time.

*Refrain*

# I Loved 'em Every One

Words and Music by Phil Sampson

recorded by T.G. Sheppard

I've known some painted ladies that sparkled in the night,
Country girls that loved the lover's moon.
Some I never really knew, though I always wanted to,
Some I only met once in a room.
Some said they liked my smile, others of 'em stayed awhile,
While others left me on the run.
This is the only way, only way I have to say,
Mm, I loved 'em ev'ry one.

*Refrain:*
Big, little, or short or tall,
Wished I could've kept them all.
Mm, I loved 'em ev'ry one.
Like to thank 'em for their charms,
Holding me in their arms,
And I hope they had some fun.

Here's to the ladies in saloons and living rooms,
Summer nights that lasted until dawn.
Here's to the memories, ev'ry one's a part of me,
Oh, I loved 'em each and ev'ry one.

*Refrain*

# I Saw the Light

Words and Music by Hank Williams

recorded by Hank Williams

I wandered so aimless, life filled with sin.
I wouldn't let my dear Savior in.
Then Jesus came like a stranger in the night.
Praise the Lord, I saw the light.

*Refrain:*
I saw the light, I saw the light.
No more darkness, no more night.
Now I'm so happy, no sorrow in sight.
Praise the Lord, I saw the light.

Just like a blind man I wandered along.
Worries and fears I claimed for my own.
Then like the blind man that God gave back his sight,
Praise the Lord, I saw the light.

*Refrain*

I was a fool to wander and stray.
Straight is the gate and narrow the way.
Now I have traded the wrong for the right.
Praise the Lord, I saw the light.

*Refrain*

# I Walk the Line

Words and Music by John R. Cash

recorded by Johnny Cash

I keep a close watch on this heart of mine.
I keep my eyes wide open all the time.
I keep the ends out for the tie that binds.
Because you're mine,
I walk the line.

I find it very, very easy to be true.
I find myself alone when each day is through.
Yes, I'll admit that I'm a fool for you.
Because you're mine,
I walk the line.

As sure as night is dark and day is light,
I keep you on my mind both day and night.
And happiness I've known proves that it's right.
Because you're mine,
I walk the line.

You've got a way to keep me on your side.
You give me a cause for love that I can't hide.
For you I know I'd even try to turn the tide.
Because you're mine,
I walk the line.

I keep a close watch on this heart of mine.
I keep my eyes wide open all of the time.
I keep the ends out for the tie that binds.
Because you're mine,
I walk the line.

# I Wish I Was Eighteen Again

Words and Music by Sonny Throckmorton

recorded by George Burns

At a bar down in Dallas, an old man chimed in,
And I thought he was out of his head;
Just being a young man, I just laughed it off
When I heard what that old man had said.

He said, "I'll never again turn the young ladies' heads
Or go running off into the wind;
I'm three-quarters home from the start to the end,
And I wish I was eighteen again.

*Refrain:*
Oh, I wish I was eighteen again
And going where I've never been.
But old folks and old oaks standing tall just pretend;
Wish I was eighteen again."

Now time turns the pages, and, oh, life goes so fast;
The years turn the black hair all gray.
I talk to some young folks; hey, they don't understand
The words this old man's got to say.

*Refrain*

Lord, I wish I was eighteen again.

# I Wanna Talk About Me

Words and Music by Bobby Braddock

recorded by Toby Keith

We talk about your work, how your boss is a jerk.
We talk about your church and your head when it hurts.
We talk about the troubles you've been havin' with your brother,
'Bout your daddy and your mother and your crazy ex-lover.
We talk about your friends and the places that you've been.
We talk about your skin and the dimples on your chin,
The polish on your toes and the run in your hose,
And God knows we're gonna talk about your clothes.
You know talkin' about you makes me smile,
But ev'ry once in a while,

*Refrain:*
I wanna talk about me. Wanna talk about I.
Wanna talk about number one, oh, my me my,
What I think, what I like, what I know, what I want, what I see.
I like talkin' about you, you, you, you usually.
But occasionally, I wanna talk about me (me me me).
I wanna talk about me.

We talk about your dreams, and we talk about your schemes,
Your high school team and your moisturizer cream.
We talk about your nanna up in Muncie, Indiana,
We talk about your grandma down in Alabama.
We talk about your guys of ev'ry shape and size,
The ones that you despise and the ones you idolize.
We talk about your heart, 'bout your brains and your smarts
And your medical charts and when you start.
You know talkin' about you makes me grin,
But ev'ry now and then,

*Refrain*

I wanna talk about me.
I wanna talk about me.
You, you, you, you,
You, you, you, you,
You, you, you, you, you,
I wanna talk about me!

*Refrain*

I wanna talk about me (me, me, me, me).
Oh, me.

# I'm So Lonesome I Could Cry

Words and Music by Hank Williams

recorded by Hank Williams and various other artists

Hear that lonesome whippoorwill,
He sounds too blue to fly.
The midnight train is whining low.
I'm so lonesome I could cry.
I've never see a night so long,
When time goes crawling by.
The moon just went behind a cloud
To hide its face and cry.

Did you ever see a robin weep
When leaves began to die.
That means he's lost the will to live.
I'm so lonesome I could cry.
The silence of a falling star
Lights up a purple sky.
And as I wonder where you are
I'm so lonesome I could cry.

# I've Got a Tiger by the Tail

Words and Music by Buck Owens and Harlan Howard

recorded by Buck Owens

*Refrain:*
I've got a tiger by the tail, it's plain to see.
I won't be much when you get through with me.
I'm-a losing weight and-a turning mighty pale,
And I know I've got a tiger by the tail.

I thought the day I met you, you were meek as a lamb;
Just the kind to fit my dreams and plans.
But now the pace we're living takes the wind from my sail,
And I know I've got a tiger by the tail.

*Refrain*

Ev'ry night you drag me where the bright lights are found.
There ain't no way to slow you down.
I'm about as helpless as a leaf in a gale,
And I know I've got a tiger by the tail.

*Refrain*

# If Drinkin' Don't Kill Me (Her Memory Will)

Words and Music by Rick Beresford and Harlan Sanders

recorded by George Jones

The bars are all closed, it's four in the morning.
Must've shut 'em all down by the shape that I'm in.
I lay my head on the wheel and the horn begins honkin',
The whole neighborhood knows I'm home drunk again.

*Refrain:*
And if drinkin' don't kill me, her memory will.
I can't hold on much longer, the way I feel.
With the blood from my body, I could start my own still.
And if drinkin' don't kill me, her memory will.

These old bones, they move slow but so sure of their footsteps,
As I trip on the floor and lightly touch down.
Lord, it's been ten bottles since I tried to forget her,
But the mem'ry still lingers lyin' here on the ground.

*Refrain*

# If I Said You Have a Beautiful Body Would You Hold It Against Me

Words and Music by David Bellamy

recorded by The Bellamy Brothers

*Refrain:*
If I said you have a beautiful body,
Would you hold it against me?
If I swore you were an angel,
Would you treat me like the devil tonight?
If I was dying on thirst,
Would your flowing love come quench me?
If I said you have a beautiful body,
Would you hold it against me?

Now, we could talk all night about the weather;
Could tell you 'bout my friends out on the coast.
I could ask a lot of crazy questions,
Or ask you what I really want to know.

*Refrain*

Now, rain can fall soft against the window;
The sun can shine so bright up in the sky.
But Daddy always told me, "Don't make small talk."
He said, "Come on out and say what's on your mind." So,

*Refrain*

# Islands in the Stream

Words and Music by Barry Gibb, Maurice Gibb and Robin Gibb

recorded by Kenny Rogers & Dolly Parton

Baby, when I met you there was peace unknown.
I set out to get you with a fine tooth comb.
I was soft inside, there was something goin' on.
You do something to me that I can't explain.
Hold me closer and I feel no pain,
Ev'ry beat of my heart, we got somethin' goin' on.
Tender love is blind, it requires a dedication.
All this love we feel needs no conversation.
We ride it together, ah ah,
Makin' love with each other, ah ah.

*Refrain:*
Islands in the stream, that is what we are,
No one in between. How can we be wrong?
Sail away with me to another world;
And we rely on each other, ah ah,
From one lover to another, ah ah.

I can't live without you if the love was gone.
Ev'rything is nothin' if you got no one.
And you did walk in the night,
Slowly losin' sight of the real thing.
But that won't happen to us, and we got no doubt,
Too deep in love and we got no way out,
And the message is clear,
This could be the year for the real thing.
No more will you cry. Baby, I will hurt you never.
We start and end as one, in love forever.
We can ride it together, ah ah,
Makin' love with each other, ah ah.

*Refrain*

# It Was Almost Like a Song

Lyric by Hal David
Music by Archie Jordan

recorded by Ronnie Milsap

Once in ev'ry life,
Someone comes along,
And you came to me.
It was almost like a song.

You were in my arms,
Just where you belong.
We were so in love.
It was almost like a song.

January through December,
We had such a perfect year.
Then the flame became a dying ember;
All at once you weren't there.

*Twice:*
Now my broken heart
Cries for you each night.
It's almost like a song,
But it's too sad to write.

It's too sad to write.

# It Wasn't God Who Made Honky Tonk Angels

Words and Music by J.D. Miller

recorded by Patsy Cline, Kitty Wells and various other artists

As I sit here tonight, the jukebox playing
The tune about the wild side of life;
As I listen to the words you are saying,
It brings mem'ries when I was a trusting wife.

*Refrain:*
It wasn't God who made honky tonk angels,
As you said in the words of your song.
Too many times married men think they're still single;
That has caused many a good girl to go wrong.

It's a shame that all the blame is on us women;
It's not true that only you men feel the same.
From the start most ev'ry heart that's ever broken
Was because there always was a man to blame.

*Refrain*

# It's a Heartache

Words and Music by Ronnie Scott and Steve Wolfe

recorded by Bonnie Tyler

It's a heartache,
Nothin' but a heartache,
Hits you when it's too late,
Hits you when you're down.
It's a fool's game,
Nothin' but a fool's game,
Standing in the cold rain,
Feeling like a clown.

It's a heartache,
Nothin' but a heartache,
Love him till your arms break,
Then he'll let you down.

It ain't right with love to share
When you find he doesn't care for you.
It ain't wise to need someone
As much as I depended on you.

*Repeat Verse 1*

It ain't right with love to share
When you find he doesn't care for you.
It ain't wise to need someone
As much as I depended on you.

It's a heartache,
Nothin' but a heartache,
You love him till your arms break,
Then he'll let you down.
It's a fool's game,
Nothin' but a fool's game,
Standing in the cold rain,
Feeling like a clown.

# It's Now or Never

Words and Music by Aaron Schroeder and Wally Gold

recorded by Elvis Presley, John Schneider

*Refrain:*
It's now or never
Come hold me tight.
Kiss me, my darlin'
Be mine tonight.
Tomorrow will be too late.
It's now or never,
My love won't wait.

When I first saw you
With your smile so tender,
My heart was captured
My soul surrendered.
I've spent a lifetime
Waiting for the right time.
Now that you're near
The time is here at last.

*Refrain*

Just like a willow
We could cry an ocean,
If we lost true love
And sweet devotion.
Your lips excite me
Let your arms invite me.
For who knows when
We'll meet again this way.

*Refrain*

# It's Your Love

Words and Music by Stephony E. Smith

recorded by Tim McGraw with Faith Hill

*Male:*
Dancin' in the dark,
Middle of the night.
Takin' your heart
And holdin' it tight.
Emotional touch
Touchin' my skin,
And askin' you to do
What you've been doin' all over again.
Oh, it's a beautiful thing.
Don't think I can keep it all in.
I just gotta let you know
What it is that won't let me go.

*Refrain:*
*Both:*
It's your love.
It just does somethin' to me
It sends a shock right through me.
I can't get enough.
And if you wonder
About the spell I'm under,
Oh, it's your love.

*Male:*
Better than I was,
More than I am,
And all of this happened
By takin' your hand.
And who I am now
Is who I wanted to be.
*Both:*
And now that we're together,
I'm stronger than ever.
I'm happy and free.
Oh, it's a beautiful thing,
Don't think I can keep it all in.
*Male:*
Oh, did you ask me why I've changed?
All I gotta do is say your sweet name.

*Both:*
*Refrain*

*Both:*
Oh, It's a beautiful thing.
Don't think I can keep it all in.
I just gotta let you know
What it is that won't let me go.

*Both:*
*Refrain*

It's your love.
It's your love.

# Jambalaya (On the Bayou)

Words and Music by Hank Williams

recorded by Hank Williams

Good-bye, Joe, me gotta go, me oh my oh.
Me gotta go pole the pirogue down the bayou.
My Yvonne, the sweetest one, me oh my oh,
Son of a gun, we'll have big fun on the bayou.

*Refrain:*
Jambalaya and a crawfish pie and fillet gumbo,
'Cause tonight I'm gonna see my ma cher amie-o.
Pick guitar, fill fruit jar, and be gay-o.
Son of a gun, we'll have big fun on the bayou.

Thibodaux, Fontaineaux, the place is buzzin'.
Kinfolk come to see Yvonne by the dozen.
Dress in style and go hog wild, me oh my oh.
Son of a gun, we'll have big fun on the bayou.

*Refrain*

Settle down far from town, get me a pirogue,
And I'll catch all the fish in the bayou.
Swap my mon to buy Yvonne what she need-o.
Son of a gun, we'll have big fun on the bayou.

*Refrain*

# Jealous Heart

Words and Music by Jenny Lou Carson

recorded by Tex Ritter, Al Morgan and various other artists

Jealous heart, oh jealous heart, stop beating.
Can't you see the damage you have done.
You have driven her away forever.
Jealous heart, now I'm the lonely one.
I was part of ev'rything she planned for,
And I know she loved me at the start.
Now she hates the sight of all I stand for.
All because of you, oh jealous heart.

You have filled my conscience full of sorrow,
For I know she never was untrue.
Jealous heart, why did you make her hate me.
Now there's nothing left but jealous you.
Many times I trusted you to guide me,
But your guiding only brought me tears.
Why, oh, why must I have you inside me,
Jealous heart, for all my lonely years.

Jealous heart, why did I let you rule me
When I knew the end would bring me pain.
Now she's gone, she's gone and found another.
Oh, I'll never see my love again.
Through the years her memory will haunt me.
Even though we're many miles apart.
It's so hard to know she'll never want me,
'Cause she heard your beating, jealous heart.

# The Keeper of the Stars

Words and Music by Karen Staley, Danny Mayo and Dickey Lee

recorded by Tracy Byrd

It was no accident, me finding you.
Someone had a hand in it long before we ever knew.
Now I just can't believe you're in my life.
Heaven's smiling down on me as I look at you tonight.

I tip my hat to the keeper of the stars.
He sure knew what he was doin'
When he joined these two hearts.
I hold everything when I hold you in my arms.
I've got all I'll ever need, thanks to the keeper of the stars.

Soft moonlight on your face, oh, how you shine.
It takes my breath away just to look into your eyes.
I know I don't deserve a treasure like you.
There really are no words to show my gratitude.

So I tip my hat to the keeper of the stars.
He sure knew what he was doin'
When he joined these two hearts.
I hold everything when I hold you in my arms.
I've got all I'll ever need, thanks to the keeper of the stars.

It was no accident, me finding you.
Someone had a hand in it long before we ever knew.

# Kentucky Rain

Words and Music by Eddie Rabbitt and Dick Heard

recorded by Elvis Presley

Seven lonely days and a dozen towns ago,
I reached out one night and you were gone.
Don't know why you'd run, what you're running to or from.
All I know is I want to bring you home.
So I'm walking in the rain, thumbing for a ride,
On this lonely Kentucky back road.
I've loved you much too long
And my love's too strong to let you go,
Never knowing what went wrong.

*Refrain:*
Kentucky rain keeps pouring down
And up ahead's another town
That I'll go walking through,
With the rain in my shoes, searchin for you.
In the cold Kentucky rain,
In the cold Kentucky rain.

Showed your photograph to some old gray-bearded men
Sitting on a bench outside a gen'ral store.
They said, "Yes, she's been here," but their mem'ry wasn't clear,
Was it yesterday, no, wait the day before.
Fin'lly got a ride with a preacher man, who asked,
"Where you bound on such a dark afternoon?"
As we drove on through the rain,
As he listened, I explained,
And he left me with a prayer that I'd find you.

*Refrain*

# King of the Road

Words and Music by Roger Miller

recorded by Roger Miller


Trailer for sale or rent,
Room to let, fifty cents.
No phone, no pool, no pets,
I ain't got no cigarettes.
Ah, but two hours of pushing broom,
Buys an eight by twelve, four bit room.
I'm a man of means by no means,
King of the road.

Third box car midnight train,
Destination Bangor, Maine.
Old worn out suit and shoes,
I don't pay no union dues.
I smoke old stogies I have found,
Short but not big around.
I'm a man of means by no means,
King of the road.

I know every engineer on every train,
All of the children and all of their names,
And every handout in every town,
And every lock that ain't locked when no one's around.

I sing trailer for sale or rent,
Rooms to let, fifty cents.
No phone, no pool, no pets,
I ain't got no cigarettes.
Ah, but two hours of pushing broom,
Buys an eight by twelve four bit room.
I'm a man of means by no means,
King of the road.

# Kiss You All Over

Words and Music by Nicky Chinn and Mike Chapman

recorded by Jim Mundy & Terri Melton

When I get home, babe, gonna light your fire.
All day I've been thinkin' about you, babe,
You're my one desire.
Gonna wrap my arms around you
And hold you close to me.
Oh, babe, I wanna taste your lips,
I wanna fill your fantasy, yeah.

I don't what I'd do without you, babe,
Don't know where I'd be.
You're not just another lover,
No, you're ev'rything to me.
Ev'ry time I'm with you, baby,
Can't believe it's true.
When you're layin' in my arms
And you do the things you do.

You can see it in my eyes, I can feel it in your touch.
You don't have to say a thing, just let me show how much
I love you, I need you, yeah.

*Refrain:*
I wanna kiss you all over and over again.
I wanna kiss you all over,
Till the night closes in,
Till the night closes in.

Stay with me, lay with me,
Holding me, loving me, baby.
Here with me, near with me,
Feeling you close to me, baby.

So show me, show me ev'rything you do,
'Cause, baby, no one does it quite like you.
I love you, I need you. Oh, babe.

*Refrain*

# The Last Cheater's Waltz

Words and Music by Sonny Throckmorton

recorded by T.G. Sheppard

She was going to pieces when he walked in the door.
She had to see him; she can't wait no more.
Tonight he'll be with her no matter the cost
As the band plays the last cheater's waltz.

He tells her he loves her and the music plays on.
He tells he needs her but someone's at home.
The ball game's all over and she knows she's lost,
As the band plays the last cheater's waltz.

*Twice:*
And ooh, don't they sound lonely?
And ooh, don't they play sad?
And ooh, three quarters only;
Watch how he holds her as they dance
To the last cheater's waltz.

# The Last Word in Lonesome Is Me

Words and Music by Roger Miller

recorded by Eddy Arnold

*Refrain:*
The last word in lonesome is me,
The last word in lonesome is me.
My heart is as lonely as a heart can be lonely,
The last word in lonesome is me.

Too bad what's happened to our good love,
Too bad what's happened to our good love.
Sometimes our best isn't quite good enough,
And the last word in lonesome is me.

*Refrain*

My heart is as lonely as a heart can be lonely,
The last word in lonesome is me.

# A Little Bitty Tear

Words and Music by Hank Cochran

recorded by Burl Ives

When you said you were leaving tomorrow,
That today was our last day;
I said there'd be no sorrow,
That I'd laugh when you walked away.

*Refrain:*
But a little bitty tear let me down,
Spoiled my act as a clown.
I had it made up not to make a frown,
But a little bitty tear let me down.

I said I'd laugh when you left me,
Pull a funny as you went out the door;
That I'd have another one waiting,
I'd wave good-bye as you go.

*Refrain*

Ev'rything went like I planned it,
And I really put on quite a show.
In my heart I felt I could stand it,
Till you walked with your grip through the door.

Then a little bitty tear let me down,
Spoiled my act as a clown.
I had it made up not to make a frown,
But a little bitty tear let me down.

# Long Gone Lonesome Blues

Words and Music by Hank Williams

recorded by Hank Williams, Hank Williams Jr.


I went down to the river to watch the fish swim by.
But I got to the river, so lonesome I wanted to die.
Oh, Lawd, and then I jumped in the river, but the doggone river was dry.
I had me a woman, she couldn't be true.
She made me for my money and she made me blue.
A man needs a woman that he can lean on,
But my leanin' post is done left and gone.
She's long gone and now I'm lonesome blues.

Gonna find me a river, one that's cold as ice.
When I find me that river, Lawd, I'm gonna pay the price.
Oh, Lawd, I'm goin' down in it three times, but I'm only comin' up twice.
She told me on a Sunday she was checkin' me out.
Along about Monday she was nowhere about.
And here it is Tuesday, ain't had no news.
Got them gone but not forgotten blues.
She's long gone and now I'm lonesome blues.

# Longneck Bottle

Words and Music by Rick Carnes and Steve Wariner

recorded by Garth Brooks

*Refrain:*
Longneck bottle, let go of my hand,
And jukebox, don't start playin' that song again.
'Cause there's a girl at home who loves me.
You know she won't understand.
Longneck bottle, let go of my hand.

Hey, barroom mirror on the wall,
Go stare at someone else.
Don't show the world the fool I am;
Just keep it to yourself.

*Refrain*

Hey, dance floor, seems you're underneath my feet
Ev'rywhere I turn.
I oughta waltz right out of them swingin' doors,
But that's a step I just can't learn.

*Refrain*

There's a girl at home who loves me.
You know she won't understand.
Longneck bottle, let go of my hand.

# Lookin' for Love

Words and Music by Wanda Mallette, Patti Ryan and Bob Morrison

from the film *Urban Cowboy*
recorded by Johnny Lee

Well, I've spent a lifetime lookin' for you;
Singles bars and good time lovers were never true.
Playin' a fool's game, hopin' to win,
And tellin' those sweet lies and losin' again.

*Refrain:*
I was lookin' for love in all the wrong places,
Lookin' for love in too many faces,
Searchin' their eyes and lookin' for traces
Of what I'm dreamin' of.
Hopin' to find a friend and a lover;
I'll bless the day I discover
Another heart lookin' for love.

And I was alone then, no love in sight;
I did ev'rything I could to get me through the night.
Don't know where it started or where it might end;
I turned to a stranger just like a friend.

*Refrain*

Then you came a-knockin' at my heart's door;
You're ev'rything I've been looking for. No more

*Repeat:*
Lookin' for love in all the wrong places,
Lookin' for love in too many faces,
Searchin' their eyes and lookin' for traces
Of what I'm dreamin' of.
Now that I've found a friend and a lover;
I bless the day I discovered
You, oh, you.

# Lost in the Fifties Tonight
## (In the Still of the Nite)

Words and Music by Mike Reid, Troy Seals and Fred Parris

recorded by Ronnie Milsap

Close your eyes, baby, follow my heart.
Call on the mem'ries here in the dark.
We'll let the magic take us away,
Back to the feeling we shared when they'd play:

*Refrain:*
In the still of the nite,
Hold me, darling, hold me tight.
Oh, shoo-doop, shoo-be doo,
Shoo-doop, doo,
So real, so right,
Lost in the fifties tonight.

These precious hours we know can't survive.
Love's all that matters while the past is alive.
Now and for always, till time disappears,
We'll hold each other whenever we hear:

*Refrain*

Shoo-doop, shoo-be doo,
Shoo-doop, shoo-be doo,
Shoo-doop, shoo-be doo,
Shoo-doop, shoo-be doo.

# Love Me Tender

Words and Music by Elvis Presley and Vera Matson

from the film *Love Me Tender*
recorded by Elvis Presley

Love me tender, love me sweet;
Never let me go.
You have made my life complete,
And I love you so.

*Refrain:*
Love me tender, love me true
All my dreams fulfill.
For, my darlin', I love you,
And I always will.

Love me tender, love me long;
Take me to your heart.
For it's there that I belong,
And we'll never part.

*Refrain*

Love me tender, love me dear;
Tell me you are mine.
I'll be yours through all the years,
Till the end of time.

*Refrain*

# Love Without End, Amen

Words and Music by Aaron G. Barker

recorded by George Strait

I got sent home from school one day with a shiner on my eye.
Fightin' was against the rules and it didn't matter why.
When Dad got home I told that story just like I'd rehearsed,
And then stood there on those tremblin' knees and waited for the worst.

And he said, "Let me tell you a secret about a father's love,
A secret that my daddy said was just between us."
He said, "Daddies don't just love their children ev'ry now and then.
It's a love without end, amen. It's a love without end, amen."

When I became a father in the spring of '81,
There was no doubt that stubborn boy was just like my father's son.
And when I thought my patience had been tested to the end,
I took my daddy's secret and I passed it on to him.

I said, "Let me tell you a secret about a father's love,
A secret that my daddy said was just between us."
I said, "Daddies don't just love their children ev'ry now and then.
It's a love without end, amen. It's a love without end, amen."

Last night I dreamed I died and stood outside those pearly gates.
When suddenly I realized there must be some mistake.
If they know half the things I've done, they'll never let me in.
And then somewhere from the other side I heard these words again.

And they said, "Let me tell you a secret about a father's love,
A secret that my daddy said was just between us.
You see, daddies don't just love their children ev'ry now and then.
It's a love without end, amen. It's a love without end, amen."

# Lucille

Words and Music by Roger Bowling and Hal Bynum

recorded by Kenny Rogers

In a bar in Toledo across from the depot,
On a bar stool she took off her ring.
I thought I'd get closer, so I walked on over,
I sat down and asked her her name.
When the drinks fin'lly hit her, she said, "I'm no quitter,
But I fin'lly quit living on dreams.
I'm hungry for laughter and here ever after,
I'm after whatever the other life brings."

In the mirror I saw him and I closely watched him,
I thought how he looked out of place.
He came to the woman who sat there beside me,
He had a strange look on his face.
The big hands were calloused, he looked like a mountain.
For a minute I thought I was dead.
But he started shaking, his big heart was breaking,
He turned to the woman and said:

*Refrain:*
You picked a fine time to leave me, Lucille,
With four hungry children and a crop in the field.
I've had some bad times, lived through some sad times,
But this time your hurtin' won't heal.
You picked a fine time to leave me, Lucille.

After he left us, I ordered more whiskey.
I thought how she made him look small.
From the lights of the barroom to a rented hotel room,
We walked without talking at all.
She was a beauty, but when she came to me,
She must've thought I'd lost my mind.
I couldn't hold her, 'cause the words that he told her
Kept coming back time after time.

*Refrain*

# Make the World Go Away

Words and Music by Hank Cochran

recorded by Eddy Arnold, Ray Price and various other artists

Do you remember when you loved me
Before the world took me astray?
If you do, then forgive me
And make the world go away.

*Refrain:*
Make the world go away
And get it off my shoulders.
Say the things you used to say
And make the world go away.

I'm sorry if I hurt you.
I'll make it up day by day.
Just say you love me like you used to
And make the world go away.

*Refrain*

# Mammas Don't Let Your Babies Grow Up to Be Cowboys

Words and Music by Ed Bruce and Patsy Bruce

featured in the film *The Electric Horseman*
recorded by Waylon Jennings & Willie Nelson

*Refrain:*
Mammas don't let your babies grow up to be cowboys.
Don't let 'em pick guitars and drive them old trucks.
Make 'em be doctors and lawyers and such.
Mammas don't let your babies grow up to be cowboys,
'Cause they'll never stay home,
And they're always alone,
Even with someone they love.

A cowboy ain't easy to love and he's harder to hold.
And it means more to him to give you a song
Than silver or gold.
Budweiser buckles and soft faded Levis
And each night begins a new day.
If you can't understand him
And he don't die young,
He'll probably just ride away.

*Refrain*

A cowboy loves smoky ole pool rooms
And clear mountain mornings.
Little warm puppies, and children, and girls of the night.
Them that don't know him won't like him,
And them that do sometimes won't know how to take him.
He's not wrong, he just different
And his pride won't let him
Do things to make you think he's right.

*Refrain*

# Me and Bobby McGee

Words and Music by Kris Kristofferson and Fred Foster

recorded by Roger Miller and various other artists

Busted flat in Baton Rouge,
Headin' for the trains,
Feelin' nearly faded as my jeans.
Bobby thumbed a diesel down
Just before it rained,
Took us all the way to New Orleans.

I took my harpoon out of my dirty red
    bandanna
And was blowin' sad while Bobby sang
    the blues.
With them windshield wipers slappin' time
And Bobby clappin' hands
We fin'lly sang up every song that driver
    knew.

Freedom's just another word for nothin'
    left to lose,
Nothin' ain't worth nothin', but it's free;
Feelin' good was easy, Lord,
When Bobby sang the blues;
And feelin' good was good enough for me,
Good enough for me and Bobby McGee.

From the coal mines of Kentucky
To the California sun,
Bobby shared the secrets of my soul;
Standin' right beside me, Lord,
Through everything I done,
And every night she kept me from the cold.

Then somewhere near Salinas, Lord,
I let her slip away
Lookin' for the home I hope she'll find.
And I'd trade all of my tomorrows
For a single yesterday,
Holdin' Bobby's body next to mine.

Freedom's just another word for nothin'
    left to lose,
Nothin' left is all she left for me;
Feelin' good was easy, Lord,
When Bobby sang the blues;
And buddy, that was good enough for me,
Good enough for me and Bobby McGee.

# Me and You and a Dog Named Boo

Words and Music by Lobo

recorded by Stonewall Jackson

I remember to this day
The bright red Georgia clay,
How it stuck to the tires after the summer rain.
Willpower made that old car go,
A woman's mind told me that it's so.
Oh, how I wish we were back on the road again.

*Refrain:*
Me and you and a dog named Boo,
Travelin' and livin' off the land.
Me and you and a dog named Boo,
How I love bein' a free man.

I can still recall
The wheatfields of St. Paul,
And the mornin' we got caught robbin' from an old hen.
Old MacDonald, he made us work,
But then he paid us for what it was worth.
Another tank of gas and back on the road again.

*Refrain*

I'll never forget that day
We motored stately into big L.A.
The lights of the city put settlin' down in my brain.
Though it's only a month or so,
That old car's buggin' us to go.
You gotta get away and get back on the road again.

*Refrain*

# My Baby Thinks He's a Train

Written by Leroy Preston

recorded by Rosanne Cash

It's 3 a.m. in the mornin',
The train whistle is blowin'.
It sounds like some lonesome song
Got in my soul, in my soul.
My baby split the blanket,
He won't be back no more.

My baby thinks he's a train.
He makes his whistle stop,
Then he's gone again.
Sometimes it's hard on a poor girl's brain, a poor girl's brain.
I'm tellin' you, boys,
My baby thinks he's a train.

*Refrain:*
Locomotion, it's the way he moves.
He drags me 'round just like an old caboose.
I'm tellin' you, girls, that man's insane.
My baby thinks he's a train.

Choo choo ain't just some train sound.
It's the noise that you hear
When my baby hits town.
With his long hair flyin',
Man, he's hard to tame.
Oh, what you s'posed to do
When your baby thinks he's a train?

He eats money like a train eats coal.
He burns it up and leaves you in the smoke.
If you wanna catch a ride,
You wait till he unwinds, he might unwind.
He's just like a train,
He always gives some tramp a ride.

*Refrain*

# My Elusive Dreams

Words and Music by Curly Putman and Billy Sherrill

recorded by David Houston & Tammy Wynette, Charlie Rich and various other artists

You followed me to Texas, you followed me to Utah,
We didn't find it there, so we moved on.
You followed me to Alabam',
Things looked good in Birmingham,
We didn't find it there, so we moved on.

*Refrain:*
I know you're tired of following
My elusive dreams and schemes,
For they're only fleeting things,
My elusive dreams.

You had my child in Memphis, I heard of work in Nashville,
We didn't find it there, so we moved on
To a small farm in Nebraska, to a gold mine in Alaska,
We didn't find it there, so we moved on.

*Refrain*

And now we've left Alaska because there was no gold mine,
But this time only two of us move on.
Now all we have is each other and a little memory to cling to,
And still you won't let me go on alone.

*Refrain*

# My Shoes Keep Walking Back to You

Words and Music by Lee Ross and Bob Wills

recorded by Ray Price

I must say that I don't care,
Hold my head up in the air,
Even tell my friends I'm glad that you don't call.
But when the day is through,
My heartache starts anew,
And that's when I miss you most of all.

*Refrain:*
And my arms keep reaching for you,
My eyes keep searching for you,
My lips keep calling for you,
And my shoes keep walking back to you.

No matter how much I pretend,
I wish I had you back again,
For nothin' else means half as much as you.
Our world just seemed to die
The day you said good-bye,
And I can't forget no matter what I do.

*Refrain*

And my shoes keep walking back to you.

# My Son Calls Another Man Daddy

Words and Music by Hank Williams and Jewell House

recorded by Hank Williams

Tonight my head is bowed in sorrow.
I can't keep the tears from my eyes.
My son calls another man Daddy.
The right to his love I've been denied.

*Refrain:*
My son calls another man Daddy.
He'll ne'er know my name or my face.
God only knows how it hurts me
For another to be in my place.

Each night I laid there in prison,
I pictured a future so bright.
And he was the one ray of sunshine
That shone through the darkness of night.

*Refrain*

Today his mother shares a new love.
She just couldn't stand my disgrace.
My son calls another man Daddy
And longs for the love he can't replace.

*Refrain*

# Ocean Front Property

Words and Music by Hank Cochran, Royce Porter and Dean Dillon

recorded by George Strait

If you leave me, I won't miss you,
And I won't ever take you back.
Girl, your mem'ry won't ever haunt me,
'Cause I don't love you. And now if you'll buy that,

*Refrain:*
I got some ocean front property in Arizona.
From my front porch you can see the sea.
I got some ocean front property in Arizona.
If you'll buy that, I'll throw the Golden Gate in free.

I don't worship the ground you walk on.
I never have, and that's a fact.
I won't follow or try to find you,
'Cause I don't love you. And now if you'll buy that,

*Refrain Twice*

If you'll buy that, I'll throw the Golden Gate in free.

# Oh, Lonesome Me

Words and Music by Don Gibson

recorded by Don Gibson and various other artists


Ev'rybody's goin' out and havin' fun.
I'm just a fool for stayin' home and havin' none.
I can't get over how she set me free.
Oh, lonesome me.

A bad mistake I'm makin' by just hangin' round.
I know that I should have some fun and paint the town.
A lovesick fool that's blind and just can't see.
Oh, lonesome me.

I'll bet she's not like me.
She's out and fancy free,
Flirting with the boys with all her charms.
But I still love her so,
And, brother, don't you know,
I'd welcome her right back here in my arms.

Well, there must be some way I can lose these lonesome blues.
Forget about the past and find somebody new.
I've thought of everything from A to Z.
Oh, lonesome me.

# Okie from Muskogee

Words and Music by Merle Haggard and Roy Edward Burris

recorded by Merle Haggard

We don't smoke marijuana in Muskogee,
And we don't take our trips on LSD.
And we don't burn our draft cards down on Main Street,
But we like living right and being free.

*Refrain:*
And I'm proud to be an Okie from Muskogee,
A place where even squares can have a ball.
We still wave Ol' Glory down at the courthouse.
White lightning's still the biggest thrill of all.

We don't make a party out of loving,
But we like holding hands and pitching woo.
We don't let our hair grow long and shaggy
Like the hippies out in San Francisco do.

*Refrain*

Leather boots are still in style if a man needs footwear.
Beads and Roman sandals won't be seen.
Football's still the roughest thing on campus,
And the kids here still respect the college dean.

*Refrain*

# Old Flames (Can't Hold a Candle to You)

Words and Music by Hugh Moffatt and Pebe Sebert

recorded by Dolly Parton and various other artists

Downtown tonight I saw an old friend, someone who
I used to take comfort from long before I met you.
I caught a spark from her eyes of forgotten desire.
With a word or a touch I could have rekindled that fire.

*Refrain:*
But old flames can't hold a candle to you.
No one can light up the night like you do.
Flickering embers of love, I've known one or two;
But old flames can't hold a candle to you.

Sometimes at night I think of old lovers I've known,
And I remember how holding them helped me not feel so alone.
When I feel you beside me and even their mem'ries are gone,
Like stars in the night lost in the sweet light of dawn.

*Refrain*

Old flames can't hold a candle to you.
Hmm.

# One Voice

Words and Music by Don Cook and David Malloy

recorded by Billy Gilman

Some kids have and some kids don't,
And some of us are wondering why.
And Mom won't watch the news at night;
There's too much stuff that's making her cry.
We need some help down here on earth.
A thousand prayers, a million words,
But one voice was heard.

A house, a yard, a neighborhood
Where you could ride your new bike to school.
A kinda world where Mom and Dad
Still believe the golden rule.
Life's not that simple down here on earth.
A thousand prayers, a million words,
But one voice was heard.

One voice, one simple word.
Hearts know what to say.
One dream can change the world.
Keep believin' till you find your way.

Yesterday while walkin' home,
I saw some kid on Newbury Road.
He pulled a pistol from his bag
And tossed it in the river below.
Thanks for the help down here on earth.
A thousand prayers, a million words,
But one voice was heard.
One voice was heard.
One voice was heard.

# Only the Lonely (Know the Way I Feel)

Words and Music by Roy Orbison and Joe Melson

recorded by Roy Orbison, Sonny James

Only the lonely know the way I feel tonight.
Only the lonely know this feeling ain't right.
There goes my baby, there goes my heart.
They've gone forever, so far apart.
But only the lonely know why I cry.
Only the lonely.

Only the lonely know the heartaches I've been through.
Only the lonely know I cry and cry for you.
Maybe tomorrow a new romance,
No more sorrow, but that's the chance
You got to take, if you're lonely heartbreak.
Only the lonely.

# Put Your Hand in the Hand

Words and Music by Gene MacLellan

recorded by Beth Moore, Anne Murray

*Refrain:*
Put your hand in the hand
Of the man who stilled the water,
Put your hand in the hand
Of the man who calmed the sea;
Take a look at yourself,
And-a you can look at others diff'rently,
By puttin' your hand in the hand
Of the man from a-Galilee.

Ev'ry time I look
Into the Holy Book, I wanna tremble
When I read about the part
Where a carpenter cleared the temple.
For the buyers and the sellers were no diff'rent fellas
Than what I profess to be,
And it causes me shame to know
I'm not the man that I should be!

*Refrain*

Mama taught me how to pray
Before I reached the age of seven.
And when I'm down on my knees
That's-a when I'm close to heaven.
Daddy lived his life with two kids and a wife
And he did what he could do,
And he showed me enough
Of what it takes to get you through.

*Refrain*

# Raining in My Heart

Words and Music by Boudleaux Bryant and Felice Bryant

recorded by Hank Williams Jr.


The sun is out, the sky is blue,
There's not a cloud to spoil the view.
But it's raining, raining in my heart.

The weatherman says, "Clear today."
He doesn't know you've gone away,
And it's raining, raining in my heart.

Oh, misery, misery.
What's gonna become of me?

I tell my blues they mustn't show,
But soon the tears are bound to flow,
'Cause it's raining, raining in my heart.

# (I'm A) Ramblin' Man

Words and Music by Ray Pennington

recorded by Waylon Jennings

I've been down the Mississippi,
Down through New Orleans. (Yes, I have.)
I've played in California,
There ain't too much I haven't seen. (Oh, yeah.)
I'm a ramblin' man,
Don't fool around with a ramblin' man.

Left a girl in West Virginia,
Up there where that green grass grows. (Yes, I did.)
Got a girl in Cincinnati
Waitin' where the Ohio River flows. (Oh, girl.)
I'm a ramblin' man,
Don't give your heart to a ramblin' man.

*Refrain:*
You'd better move away,
You're standin' too close to the flame,
Once I mess with your mind
Your little heart won't be the same.
I'm a ramblin' man,
Don't mess around with any old ramblin' man.

Well, up in Chicago
I was known as quite a boy. (Yes, I was.)
Down in Alabama
They call me the man of joy. (Still do.)
I'm a ramblin' man,
Don't fall in love with a ramblin' man.

*Refrain*

# Release Me

Words and Music by Robert Yount, Eddie Miller and Dub Williams

recorded by Ray Price, Kitty Wells and various other artists

Please release me, let me go,
For I don't love you anymore.
To waste our lives would be a sin;
Release me and let me love again.

I have found a new love, dear,
And I will always want her near.
Her lips are warm while yours are cold;
Release me, my darling, let me go.

Please release me, can't you see
You'd be a fool to cling to me?
To live a lie would bring us pain,
So release me and let me love again.

# Ring of Fire

Words and Music by Merle Kilgore and June Carter

recorded by Johnny Cash

Love is a burning thing
And it makes its fiery ring
Bound by wild desires,
I fell into a ring of fire.

*Refrain:*
I fell into a burning ring of fire
I went down, down, down
And the flames went higher.
And it burns, burns, burns,
The ring of fire,
The ring of fire.

The taste of love is sweet
When hearts like ours beat.
I fell for you like a child,
Oh, but the fire went wild.

*Refrain*

*Repeat and Fade:*
And it burns, burns, burns,
The ring of fire,
The ring of fire.

# Rocky Top

Words and Music by Boudleaux Bryant and Felice Bryant

recorded by Lynn Anderson and various other artists


Wish that I was on ol' Rocky Top,
Down in the Tennessee hills.
Ain't no smoggy smoke on Rocky Top;
Ain't no telephone bills.
Once I had a girl on Rocky Top,
Half bear, other half cat;
Wild as a mink but sweet as soda pop,
I still dream about that.

*Refrain:*
Rocky Top, you'll always be
Home sweet home to me.
Good ol' Rocky Top,
Rocky Top, Tennessee,
Rocky Top, Tennessee.

Once two strangers climbed ol' Rocky Top,
Lookin' for a moonshine still.
Strangers ain't come down from Rocky Top;
Reckon they never will.
Corn won't grow at all on Rocky Top;
Dirt's too rocky by far.
That's why all the folks on Rocky Top
Get their corn from a jar.

*Refrain*

I've had years of cramped-up city life,
Trapped like a duck in a pen.
All I know is it's a pity life
Can't be simple again.

*Refrain*

# Saginaw, Michigan

Words and Music by Don Wayne and Bill Anderson

recorded by Lefty Frizzell

I was born in Saginaw, Michigan.
I grew up in a house on Saginaw Bay.
My dad was a poor hardworking Saginaw fisherman.
Too many times he came home with too little pay.

I loved a girl in Saginaw, Michigan,
The daughter of a wealthy, wealthy man.
But he called me that son of a Saginaw fisherman,
Not good enough to claim his daughter's hand.

Now I'm up here in Alaska looking around for gold.
Like a crazy fool I'm digging in this frozen ground so cold.
But with each new day I pray I'll strike it rich, and then
I'll go back home and claim my love in Saginaw, Michigan.

I wrote my love in Saginaw, Michigan,
I said, "Honey, I'm coming home. Please wait for me.
You can tell your dad I'm coming back a richer man.
I hit the biggest strike in Klondike history."

Her dad met me in Saginaw, Michigan.
He gave me a great big party with Champagne.
Then he said, "Son, you're a wise, young, ambitious man.
Will you sell your father-in-law your Klondike claim?"

Now he's up there in Alaska digging in the cold, cold ground.
The greedy fool is looking for the gold I never found.
It serves him right, and no one here is missing him,
Least of all the newlyweds of Saginaw, Michigan.

# Sail Away

Words and Music by Rafe VanHoy

recorded by The Oak Ridge Boys

Across the bay a lady waits to hold me tight,
And my boat and I are ready to set sail.
If the weather keeps on holdin' and the wind is right,
I'll be wrapped up in my sweet one's arms tonight.

*Refrain:*
And we will sail away on the wings of love into the night,
Cast out our fortunes on the sea.
Then we will go to sleep together with the rocking of the water,
And dream of how our life will someday be,
When she sails away with me.

As I skip across the waves, my sails are high and full,
My mind is on the one I wait to see.
And I dream about an island somewhere in my mind,
Where someday I will take her off with me.

*Refrain*

Then a smile comes upon me as I look across the bow.
I see a lady on the side.
But she will wait no more as I head for the shore,
'Cause tonight I'm gonna take her for a ride.

*Refrain*

# Send Me the Pillow You Dream On

Words and Music by Hank Locklin

recorded by Hank Locklin and various other artists

Send me the pillow that you dream on,
Don't you know that I still care for you?
Send me the pillow that you dream on,
So, darling, I can dream on it too.

Each night while I'm sleeping, oh, so lonely,
I'll share your love in dreams that once were true.
Send me the pillow that you dream on,
So, darling, I can dream on it too.

I've waited so long for you to write me,
But just a mem'ry's all that's left of you.
Send me the pillow that you dream on,
So, darling, I can dream on it too.

# Shadows in the Moonlight

Words and Music by Charlie Black and Rory Bourke

recorded by Anne Murray

*Refrain:*
We'll be shadows in the moonlight.
Darling, I'll meet you at midnight,
Hand in hand we'll go
Dancin' through the Milky Way.

And we'll find a little hideaway
Where we can love the whole night away.
We'll be shadows in the moonlight
Right up till the light of day.

Ooh, the night is young,
And baby, so are we.
Glad, I'm gonna make you glad you came.
Ooh, you won't need a thing,
Just bring your love for me,
And darlin', I will do the same.

*Refrain*

Ooh, you won't need a thing,
Just bring your love for me.
You'll be glad you came, just wait and see, wait and see.

*Refrain*

And we'll find a little hideaway
Where we can love the whole night away.
We'll be shadows in the moonlight
Right up till the light of day.

# Shameless

Words and Music by Billy Joel

recorded by Garth Brooks

Well, I'm shameless when it comes to
  loving you.
I'd do anything you want me to.
I'd do anything at all.
And I'm standing here for all the world
  to see.
Ah, there ain't that much left of me
That has very far to fall.
You know, I'm not a man who's ever been
Insecure about the world I've been living in.
I don't break easy. I have my pride.
But if you need to be satisfied,

I'm shameless. Baby, I don't have a prayer.
Anytime I see you standing there,
I go down upon my knees.
And I'm changing. I swore I'd never
  compromise.
Ah, but you convinced me otherwise.
I'll do anything you please.
You see, in all my life I've never found
What I couldn't resist, what I couldn't turn
  down.
I could walk away from anyone I ever knew,
But I can't walk away from you.

I have never let anything have this much
  control over me.
I worked too hard to call my life my own.
Well, I made myself a world, and it worked
  so perfectly.
But it's your world now. I can't refuse.
I never had so much to lose.
I'm shameless.

You know, it should be easy for a man who's
  strong
To say he's sorry or admit where he's wrong.
I've never lost anything I ever missed,
But I've never been in love like this.
It's out of my hands.

I'm shameless. I don't have the power now.
But I don't want it anyhow.
So I've got to let it go.
I'm shameless, shameless as a man can be.
You can make a total fool of me.
I just wanted you to know
I'm shameless.

# She's Got You

Words and Music by Hank Cochran

recorded by Patsy Cline, Loretta Lynn

I've got your picture that you gave to me,
And it's signed "with love" just like it used to be.
The only thing diff'rent, the only thing new,
I've got your picture, she's got you.

I've got the records that we used to share,
And they still sound the same as when you were here.
The only thing diff'rent, the only thing new,
I've got the records, she's got you.

*Bridge:*
I've got your memory, or has it got me?
I really don't know, but I know
It won't let me be.

I've got your class ring that proved you cared.
And it still looks the same as when you gave it, dear.
The only thing diff'rent, the only thing new,
I've got these little things, she's got you.

*Repeat Bridge and Last Verse*

# She's Not the Cheatin' Kind

Words and Music by Ronnie Dunn

recorded by Brooks & Dunn

She's dressed to kill in a dress that he bought her.
She wouldn't care if he walked in and caught her.
She's come to dance a dance or two
And do no tellin' what by the time the night is through.

She found out the hard way about him.
She's out to find out how she'll do without him.
Her hands are shakin', her heart's poundin'.
By the way she's drinkin', his mem'ry's drownin'.

*Refrain:*
She's not the cheatin' kind.
She's been cheated one too many times.
Oh, she's never fooled around.
He's still lyin'. She's through cryin'.
She's not foolin' now.

She walks by and ev'ry head turns.
You can see how high her fire burns.
He didn't know what a good thing he had.
Well, it's too late. Well, that's too bad, 'cause

*Refrain Twice*

# Singing the Blues

Words and Music by Melvin Endsley

recorded by Marty Robbins and various other artists

Well I never felt more like singing the blues
'Cause I never thought that I'd ever lose your love, dear,
Why'd you do me this way?

Well, I never felt more like crying all night
'Cause everything's wrong and nothing's right without you.
You got me singing the blues.

The moon and stars no longer shine,
The dream is gone I thought was mine.
There's nothing left for me to do but cry over you.

Well, I never felt more like running away
But why should I go 'cause I couldn't stay without you.
You got me singing the blues.

# Sixteen Tons

Words and Music by Merle Travis

recorded by Tennessee Ernie Ford

Some people say a man is made out of mud
A poor man's made out of muscle and blood,
Muscle and blood and skin and bones,
A mind that's weak and back that's strong.

*Refrain:*
You load sixteen tons. What do you get?
Another day older and deeper in debt.
Saint Peter, don't you call me 'cause I can't go
I owe my soul to the company store.

I was born one mornin' when the sun didn't shine
I picked up my shovel and I walked to the mine,
I loaded sixteen tons of number nine coal.
And the straw boss said, "Well-a bless my soul."

*Refrain*

I was born one mornin', it was drizzling rain
Fightin' and trouble are my middle name.
I was raised in a cane brake by an ole mama lion.
Cain't no hightoned woman make me walk the line.

*Refrain*

If you see me comin' better step aside
A lotta men didn't, a lotta men died.
One first of iron, the other of steel.
If the right one don't-a get you, then the left one will.

*Refrain*

# Skip a Rope

Words and Music by Jack Moran and Glenn D. Tubb

recorded by Henson Cargill

*Refrain:*
Skip a rope, skip a rope,
Oh, listen to the children while they play.
Now ain't it kinda funny what the children say?
Skip a rope.

Daddy hates Mommy, Mommy hates Dad;
Last night you should've heard the fight they had.
It gave little sister another bad dream;
She woke us all up with a terrible scream.

*Refrain*

Cheat on your taxes, don't be a fool;
What was that they said about the Golden Rule?
Well, never mind the rules, just play to win,
And hate your neighbor for the shade of his skin.

*Refrain*

Stab him in the back, that's the name of the game,
And Mommy and Daddy are who's to blame.

Skip a rope, skip a rope,
Just listen to your children while they play.
It's really not very funny what the children say.
Skip a rope.

# Snowbird

Words and Music by Gene MacLellan

recorded by Anne Murray


Beneath this snowy mantle cold and clean,
The unborn grass lies waiting for its coat to turn to green.
The snowbird sings the song he always sings
And speaks to me of flowers that will bloom again in spring.

When I was young, my heart was young then too,
And anything that it would tell me, that's the thing that I would do.
But now I feel such emptiness within,
For the thing I want the most in life is the thing that I can't win.

Spread your tiny wings and fly away,
And take the snow back with you where it came from on that day.
The one I love forever is untrue,
And if I could, you know I that would fly away with you.

The breeze along the river seems to say
That he'll only break my heart again should I decide to stay.
So little snowbird, take me with you when you go
To that land of gentle breezes where the peaceful waters flow.

Yeah, if I could, you know that I would fly away with you.

# Some Days Are Diamonds
## (Some Days Are Stone)

Words and Music by Dick Feller

recorded by John Denver

When you ask how I've been here without you,
I'd like to say I've been fine, and I do.
But we both know the truth is hard to come by,
And if I told the truth, that's not quite true.

*Refrain:*
Some days are diamonds, some days are stone.
Sometimes the hard times won't leave me alone.
Sometimes the cold wind blows a chill in my bones.
Some days are diamonds, some days are stone.

Now the face that I see in my mirror,
More and more is a stranger to me.
More and more I can see there's a danger
In becoming what I never thought I'd be.

*Refrain*

# Somebody's Knockin'

Words and Music by Ed Penney and Jerry Gillespie

recorded by Terri Gibbs

Somebody's knockin', should I let him in?
Lord, it's the devil, would you look at him.
I've heard about him but I never dreamed
He'd have blue eyes and blue jeans.

Well, somebody's talkin', he's whispering to me,
Your place or my place, well, which will it be?
I'm gettin' weaker and he's comin' on strong,
But I don't wanna go wrong.

He must have tapped my telephone line.
He must have known I'm spendin' my time alone.
He says we'll have one heavenly night.
My fever's burnin', so he oughta be right at home.

*Repeat Verse 1*

He must have tapped my telephone line.
He must have known I'm spendin' my time alone.
He says we'll have one heavenly night.
My fever's burnin', so he oughta be right at home.

Somebody's knockin',
Somebody's knockin',
Um, somebody's knockin'.

# Son-of-a-Preacher Man

Words and Music by John Hurley and Ronnie Wilkins

recorded by Dusty Springfield and various other artists

Jimmy Ray was a preacher's son.
When his daddy would visit he'd come along.
When they gathered 'round
the parlor talkin',
Cousin Jimmy would take me walkin'.
Out through the backyard we'd go walkin',
And then he'd look into my eyes,
Lord knows, to my surprise.

*Refrain:*
The only one who could ever reach me
Was the son of a preacher man.
The only boy who could ever teach me
Was the son of a preacher man,
Yes he was, he was, ooh.

Bein' good isn't always easy,
No matter how hard I try.
When he started sweet talkin' to me,
He'd come 'n' tell me ev'rything is alright,
Kiss and tell me ev'rything is alright
And "Can I get away again tonight."

*Refrain*

How well I remember
The look that was in his eyes,
Stealin' kisses from me on the sly,
Takin' time to make time,
Tellin' me that he's all mine.
Learnin' from each other's knowin'
And lookin' to see how much we've grown.

And the only one who could ever reach me
Was the son of a preacher man.
The only one who could ever teach me
Was the son of a preacher man.
Yes, he was. Yeah!

# The Song Remembers When

Words and Music by Hugh Prestwood

recorded by Trisha Yearwood

I was standing at the counter,
I was waiting for the change,
When I heard that old familiar music start.
It was like a lighted match
Had been tossed into my soul.
It was like a dam had broken in my heart.
After taking ev'ry detour,
Getting lost and losing track,
So that even if I wanted,
I could not find my way back;
After driving out the mem'ry
Of the way things might've been,
After I've forgotten all about us,
The song remembers when.

We were rolling through the Rockies,
We were up above the clouds,
When a station out of Jackson played
   that song.
And it seemed to fit the moment,
And the moment seemed to freeze,
When we turned the music up and
   sang along.
And there was a God in Heaven,
And the world made perfect sense.
We were young and were in love,
And we were easy to convince.
We were heading straight for Eden.
It was just around the bend,
And though I have forgotten all about it,
The song remembers when.

I guess something must've happened,
And we must've said good-bye.
And my heart must have been broken,
Though I can't recall just why.
The song remembers when.

Oh, for all the miles between us
And for all the time that's passed,
You would think I haven't gotten very far.
And I hope my hasty heart
Would forgive me just this once,
If I stop to wonder how on earth you are.
But that's just a lot of water
Underneath the bridge I burned,
And there's no use in backtracking
Around corners I have turned.
Still, I guess some things we bury
Are just bound to rise again,
For even if the whole world has forgotten,
The song remembers when.
Yeah, and even if the whole world has
   forgotten,
The song remembers when.

# Southern Nights

Words and Music by Allen Toussaint

recorded by Glen Campbell

Southern nights, have you ever felt a southern night?
Free as a breeze, not to mention the trees,
Whistling tunes that you know and love so.
Southern nights, just as good even when closed your eyes.
I apologize to anyone who can truly say
That he has found a better way.

Southern skies, have you ever noticed southern skies?
Its precious beauty lies just beyond the eye.
It goes running through your soul like the stories told of old.
Old man, he and his dog that walked the old land,
Ev'ry flower touched his cold hand. As he slowly walked by,
Weeping willows would cry for joy.

Feel so good, feel so good, it's fright'ning.
Wish I could stop this world from fighting.
La da da da da da,
La da da da da da,
Da da da da da
Da da da da da da.

Mysteries like this and many others in the trees
Blow in the night in the southern skies.

# Stand by Me

Words and Music by Ben E. King, Jerry Leiber and Mike Stoller

recorded by Ben E. King, Mickey Gilley
featured in the film *Stand by Me*

When the night has come and the land is dark
And the moon is the only light we'll see.
No I won't be afraid, no I won't be afraid
Just as long as you stand,
Stand by me.

*Refrain:*
So darling, darling,
Stand by me,
Oh, stand by me,
Oh, stand,
Stand by me,
Stand by me.

If the sea that we look upon should tumble and fall
Or the mountain crumble in the sea.
I won't cry, no I won't shed a tear
Just as long as you stand
Stand by me.

*Refrain*

Whenever you're in trouble won't you stand by me
Oh, stand by me,
Oh, stand by me,
Stand by me.

*Refrain*

# Sweet Dreams

Words and Music by Don Gibson

recorded by Patsy Cline, Faron Young, Don Gibson, Emmylou Harris and various other artists

Sweet dreams of you,
Ev'ry night I go through.
Why can't I forget you and start my life anew
Instead of having sweet dreams about you.

*Refrain:*
You don't love me, it's plain.
I should know you'll never wear my name.
I should hate you the whole night through
Instead of having sweet dreams about you.

Sweet dreams of you,
Things I know can't come true.
Why can't I forget the past,
Start loving someone new,
Instead of having sweet dreams about you.

*Refrain*

# Tennessee Waltz

Words and Music by Redd Stewart and Pee Wee King

recorded by Patti Page, Pee Wee King and various other artists

I was waltzing with my darlin'
To the Tennessee waltz,
When an old friend I happened to see.

Introduced him to my loved one
And while they were waltzing,
My friend stole my sweetheart from me.

I remember the night and the Tennessee Waltz.
Now I know just how much I have lost.
Yes, I lost my little darlin' the night they were playing
The beautiful Tennessee Waltz.

# Thank God and Greyhound

Words and Music by Larry Kingston and Ed Nix

recorded by Roy Clark

I've made a small fortune and you've squandered it all.
You shamed me till I feel about one inch tall.
But I thought I loved you and I hoped you would change.
So I gritted my teeth and I didn't complain.

Now you come to me with a simple good-bye.
You tell me you're leaving, but you don't tell me why.
Now we're here at the station, and you're getting on.
And all I can think of is, thank God and Greyhound, you're gone.

Thank God and Greyhound, you're gone.
I didn't know how much longer I could go on,
Watching you take the respect out of me,
Watching you make a total wreck out of me.
That big diesel motor is a-playing my song.
Thank God and Greyhound, you're gone.

Thank God and Greyhound, you're gone.
The load on my mind got lighter when you got on.
That shiny old bus is a beautiful sight.
With the black smoke a-rollin' up around the tail lights.
It may sound kinda cruel, but I've been silent too long.
Thank God and Greyhound, you're gone.
Thank God and Greyhound, you're gone.

# Thank God I'm a Country Boy

Words and Music by John Martin Sommers

recorded by John Denver

Well, life on a farm is kinda laid back.
Ain't much an old country boy like me can't hack.
It's early to rise, early in the sack.
Thank God I'm a country boy.
A simple kinda life never did me no harm,
Raisin' me a family and workin' on a farm.
My days are filled with an easy country charm.
Thank God I'm a country boy.

*Refrain:*
Well, I got me a fine wife, I got me old fiddle.
When the sun's comin' up I got cakes on the griddle.
And life ain't nothin' but a funny, funny riddle.
Thank God I'm a country boy.

When the work's all done and the sun's settin' low,
I pull out my fiddle and I rosin up the bow.
But the kids are asleep so I keep it kinda low.
Thank God I'm a country boy.
I'd play "Sally Goodin'" all day if I could,
But the Lord and my wife wouldn't take it very good.
So I fiddle when I can and I work when I should.
Thank God I'm a country boy.

*Refrain*

I wouldn't trade my life for diamonds or jewels.
I never was one of them money-hungry fools.
I'd rather have my fiddle and my farmin' tools.
Thank God I'm a country boy.
Yeah, city folk drivin' in a black limousine,
A lotta sad people thinkin' that's mighty keen.
Well, folks, let me tell you now exactly what I mean:
I thank God I'm a country boy.

*Refrain*

Well, my fiddle was my daddy's till the day he died,
And he took me by the hand and held me close to his side.
He said, "Live a good life and play my fiddle with pride,
And thank God you're a country boy."
My daddy taught me young how to hunt and how to whittle.
He taught me how to work and play a tune on the fiddle.
He taught me how to love and how to give just a little.
Thank God I'm a country boy.

*Refrain*

# There's a Tear in My Beer

Words and Music by Hank Williams

recorded by Hank Williams Jr. and Hank Williams

There's a tear in my beer 'cause I'm cryin' for you, dear,
You are on my lonely mind.
Into these last few beers I have shed a million tears.
You are on my lonely mind.
I'm gonna keep drinkin' until I'm petrified,
And then maybe these tears will leave my eyes.
There's a tear in my beer 'cause I'm cryin' for you, dear.
You are on my lonely mind.

Last night I walked the floor and the night before.
You are on my lonely mind.
It seems my life is through and I'm so doggone blue.
You are on my lonely mind.
I'm gonna keep drinkin' till I can't move a toe,
And then maybe my heart won't hurt me so.
There's a tear in my beer 'cause I'm cryin' for you, dear.
You are on my lonely mind.

Lord, I've tried and I've tried, but my tears I can't hide.
You are on my lonely mind.
All these blues that I've found have really got me down.
You are on my lonely mind.
I'm gonna keep drinkin' till I can't even think,
'Cause in the last week I ain't slept a wink.
There's a tear in my beer 'cause I'm cryin' for you, dear.
You are on my lonely mind.

# Through the Years

Words and Music by Steve Dorff and Marty Panzer

recorded by Kenny Rogers

I can't remember when you weren't there,
When I didn't care for anyone but you,
I swear we've been through everything there is,
Can't imagine anything we've missed.
Can't imagine anything the two of us can't do.

Through the years
You've never let me down,
You've turned my life around.
The sweetest days I've found
I've found with you.

Through the years,
I've never been afraid,
I've loved the life we've made,
And I'm so glad I've stayed
Right here with you
Through the years.

I can't remember what I used to do,
Who I trusted
Who I listened to before.
I swear you've taught me everything I know,
Can't imagine needing someone so.

Through the years,
I've never been afraid,
I've loved the life we've made,
And I'm so glad I've stayed
Right here with you
Through the years.

# The Tip of My Fingers

Words and Music by Bill Anderson

recorded by Eddy Arnold, Bill Anderson, Steve Wariner and various other artists

I reached out my arms and I touched you,
With soft words I whispered your name.
I held you right on the tip of my fingers,
But that was as close as I came.

My eyes had a vision of sweet lips,
Yielding beneath my command.
I had your love on the tip of my fingers,
But I let it slip right through my hands,
But I let it slip right through my hands.

Somebody took you when I wasn't looking,
And I should have known from the start.
It's a long, long way from the tip of my fingers
To the love hidden deep in your heart,
To the love hidden deep in your heart.

# Wake Up Little Susie

Words and Music by Boudleaux Bryant and Felice Bryant

recorded by The Everly Brothers

Wake up, little Susie, wake up.
Wake up, little Susie, wake up.

We've both been sound asleep,
Wake up, little Susie and weep.
The movie's over, it's four o'clock,
And we're in trouble deep.

*Refrain:*
Wake up, little Susie, wake up little Susie,
Well, what are we gonna tell your Mama?
What are we gonna tell your Pa?
What are we gonna tell our friends when they say,
"Ooh la la"
Wake up, little Susie, wake up, little Susie.

Well, we told your Mama that we'd be in by ten.
Well, Susie baby, looks like we goofed again
Wake up, little Susie, wake up, little Susie
We've gotta go home.

The movie wasn't so hot,
It didn't have much of a plot.
We fell asleep, and our goose is cooked,
Our reputation is shot.

*Refrain*

# Walkin' After Midnight

Lyrics by Don Hecht
Music by Alan W. Block

recorded by Patsy Cline

I go out walkin' after midnight
In the moonlight, just like we used to do.
I'm always walkin' after midnight searchin' for you.

I'll walk for miles along the highway,
That's just my way of being close to you.
I go out walkin' after midnight searchin' for you.

I stop to see a weepin' willow,
Cryin' on his pillow,
Maybe he's cryin' for me.
And as the sky turns gloomy,
Night winds whisper to me.
I'm lonely as lonely can be.

I'll go out walkin' after midnight
In the starlight and pray that you may be
Somewhere just walkin' after midnight searchin' for me.

# Walking in the Sunshine

Words and Music by Roger Miller

recorded by Roger Miller

Walkin' in the sunshine, sing a little sunshine song.
Put a smile upon your face as if there's nothing wrong.
Think about a good time had a long time ago;
Think about forgetting about your worries and your woes.
Walkin' in the sunshine, sing a little sunshine song.

La la la la la dee oh,
Whether the weather be rain or snow,
Pretending can make it real;
A snowy pasture, a green and grassy field.

*Repeat Verse 1*

# Walking on New Grass

Words and Music by Ray Pennington

recorded by Kenny Price

I'm like a cloud drifting from town to town,
Each new love just helps me on my way.
No one woman's ever gonna tie me down,
When one gets too close I just back up and say:

*Refrain:*
Got to be walking on new grass, singing a new song,
Tomorrow there's no telling where I'll be.
But I'll be walking on new grass, singing a new song,
The next town up the road keeps calling me.

I'm warning you, don't fall in love with me,
I don't plan on being here too long.
You're just a leaf caught in a playful breeze,
I'll carry you a while, then I'll be moving on.

*Refrain*

I won't take roots, I never stay that long,
And a bad seed just won't grow anyway.
This rolling stone don't want to gather no moss,
So when the grass starts to grow, then I'll be on my way.

*Refrain*

# Walking the Floor Over You

Words and Music by Ernest Tubb

recorded by George Hamilton IV, Ernest Tubb

You left me and you went away.
You said that you'd be back in just a day.
You've broken your promise and you left me here alone,
I don't know why you did,
Dear but I know that you're gone.

*Refrain:*
I'm walking the floor over you.
I can't sleep a wink that is true.
I'm hoping and I'm praying as my heart breaks right in two.
Walking the floor over you.

Darling, you know I love you well,
Love you more than I can ever tell.
I thought that you wanted me and always would be mine,
But you went and left me here with troubles on my mind.

*Refrain*

Now, someday you may be lonesome too,
Walking the floor is good for you.
Just keep right on walking and it won't hurt you to cry,
Remember that I love you and I will the day I die.

*Refrain*

# The Way You Love Me

Words and Music by Michael Dulaney and Keith Follese

recorded by Faith Hill


If I could grant you one wish,
I'd wish you could see the way you kiss.
Ooh, I love watching you, baby,
When you're driving me, ooh, crazy.

*Refrain:*
Ooh, I love the way you,
Love the way you love me.
There's nowhere else I'd rather be.
Ooh, to feel the way I feel with your arms around me.
I only wish that you could see the way you love me.
Whoa oh oh, the way you love me.

It's not right, it's not fair,
What you're missing over there.
Someday I'll find a way to show you
Just how lucky I am to know you.

*Refrain*

You're the million reasons why
There's love reflecting in my eyes.

*Refrain*

Whoa oh oh, the way you love me.
Whoa oh oh, the way you love me.
Oh, the way you love me.
The way you love me.
Ooh, I love the way you love me. Oh yeah.
Ooh, I love the way you love me. Oh yeah.

# Welcome to My World

Words and Music by Ray Winkler and John Hathcock

recorded by Jim Reeves, Eddy Arnold


Welcome to my world,
Won't you come on in?
Miracles, I guess,
Still happen now and then.
Step into my heart,
Leave your cares behind,
Welcome to my world,
Built with you in mind.
Knock and the door will open,
Seek and you will find,
Ask and you'll be given
The key to this world of mine.
I'll be waiting here
With my arms unfurled,
Waiting just for you,
Welcome to my world.

# What Are We Doin' in Love

Words and Music by Randy Goodrum

recorded by Dottie West with Kenny Rogers

We're like summer and winter.
We're not one bit alike.
We're like satin and cinders.
I'm definitely not your type.

Well then, what are we doin' in love?
What are we doin' in a mess like this?
What are we doin' in love?
Why were you someone I couldn't resist?
What are we doin' in love?

We're like paper and matches.
We'll prob'ly have our share of fights.
We're like roses and switches.
It's gonna be hard, but we've got to try.

Oh, what are we doin' in love?
What are we doin' in a mess like this?
What are we doin' in love?
What are we gonna tell all our friends?

You don't have to like someone to love
    someone.
That rule was made to be broken.
But if we have to say good-bye to a life
    we've gotten used to,
What are we doin' in love then?

We're like sunup and sundown.
People say we're never gonna last.
We're like uptown and downtown.
You like it slow and I like it fast.

So what are we doin' in love?
What are we doin' in a mess like this?
What are we doin' in love?
What are we gonna tell all our friends?
What are we doin' in love?
What are we doin' in a mess like this?
What are we doin' in love?
What are we gonna tell all our friends?
That's what we're doin' in love.

# What's Forever For

Words and Music by Rafe VanHoy

recorded by Michael Martin Murphey

I've been looking at people
And how they change with the times;
And lately all I've been seeing are people
Throwing love away and losing their minds.

Maybe it's me who's gone crazy,
But I can't understand why
All these lovers keep hurting each other,
When good love is so hard to come by.

*Refrain:*
So what's the glory in living?
Doesn't anybody ever stay together anymore?
And if love never lasts forever,
Tell me: what's forever for?

And I see love-hungry people
Trying their best to survive;
When right there in their hands is a dying romance,
And they're not even trying to keep it alive.

*Refrain Twice*

# When Will I Be Loved

Words and Music by Phil Everly

recorded by Linda Ronstadt

I've been cheated,
Been mistreated;
When will I be loved?

I've been pushed down,
I've been pushed 'round;
When will I be loved?

When I find my new man
That I want for mine,
He always breaks my heart in two;
It happens ev'ry time.

I've been made blue,
I've been lied to;
When will I be loved?

When I find my new man
That I want for mine,
He always breaks my heart in two;
It happens every time.

I've been cheated,
Been mistreated;
When will I be loved?
When will I be loved?
Tell me, when will I be loved?

# When You Say Nothing at All

Words and Music by Paul Overstreet and Don Schlitz

recorded by Keith Whitley, Alison Krauss & Union Station
featured in the film *Notting Hill*

It's amazing how you can speak right to my heart.
Without saying a word you can light up the dark.
Try as I may I could never explain
What I hear when you don't say a thing.

*Refrain:*
The smile on your face lets me know that you need me.
There's truth in your eyes saying you'll never leave me.
A touch of your hand says you'll catch me if ever I fall.
Now you say it's best when you say nothing at all.

All day long I can hear people talking out loud,
But when you hold me near you drown out the crowd.
Old Mister Webster could never define
What's being said between your heart and mine.

*Refrain*

# Where the Stars and Stripes and Eagle Fly

Words and Music by Aaron Tippin, Casey Beathard and Kenny Beard

recorded by Aaron Tippin


Well, if you ask me where I come from,
Here's what I tell ev'ryone.
I was born by God's dear grace
In an extraordinary place
Where the stars and stripes and the eagle fly.

It's a big ol' land with countless dreams,
And happiness ain't out of reach.
Hard work pays off the way it should.
Yeah, I've seen enough to know that we've got it good
Where the stars and stripes and the eagle fly.

There's a lady that stands in a harbor
For what we believe.
And there's a bell that still echoes
The price that it cost to be free.

I pledge allegiance to this flag,
And if that bothers you, well, that's too bad.
But if you got pride and you're proud you do,
Hey, we could use some more like me and you
Where the stars and stripes and the eagle fly.

There's a lady that stands in a harbor
For what we believe.
And there's a bell that still echoes
The price that it cost to be free.

No, it ain't the only place on earth,
But it's the only place that I prefer
To love my wife and raise my kids,
Hey, the same way that my daddy did:
Where the stars and stripes and the eagle fly.
Where the stars and stripes and the eagle fly.

# Where've You Been

Words and Music by Don Henry and Jon Vezner

recorded by Kathy Mattea

Claire had all but given up
When she and Edwin fell in love.
She touched his face and shook her head
In disbelief. She sighed and said,
"In many dreams I've held you near,
But now at last you're really here."

*Refrain:*
Where have you been?
I've looked for you forever and a day.
Where have you been?
I'm just not myself when you're away.

He asked her for her hand for life,
And she became a salesman's wife.
He was home each night by eight,
But one stormy evening he was late.
Her frightened tears fell to the floor
Until his key turned in the door.

*Refrain*

They'd never spent a night apart.
For sixty years she heard him snore.
Now they're in a hospital
In sep'rate beds on diff'rent floors.

Claire soon lost her memory;
Forgot the names of family.
She never spoke a word again.
Then one day, they wheeled him in.
He held her hand and stroked her head.
In a fragile voice she said,

*Refrain*

No, I'm just not myself when you're away.

# Where Were You
## (When the World Stopped Turning)

Words and Music by Alan Jackson

recorded by Alan Jackson


Where were you when the world stopped turnin'
That September day?
Out in the yard with your wife and children
Or workin' on some stage in L.A.?
Did you stand there in shock at the sight of that black smoke
Risin' against that blue sky?
Did you shout out in anger, in fear for your neighbor,
Or did you just sit down and cry?

Did you weep for the children, they lost their dear loved ones,
Pray for the ones who don't know?
Did you rejoice for the people who walked from the rubble
And sob for the ones left below?
Did you burst out in pride for the red, white, and blue
And heroes who died just doin' what they do?
Did you look up to heaven for some kind of answer
And look at yourself and what really matters?

*Refrain:*
I'm just a singer of simple songs.
I'm not a real political man.
I watch CNN, but I'm not sure I can tell you
The diff'rence in Iraq and Iran.
But I know Jesus and I talk to God,
And I remember this from when I was young:
Faith, hope, and love are some good things He gave us
And the greatest is love.

Where were you when the world stopped turnin'
That September day?
Teachin' a class full of innocent children
Or drivin' on some cold interstate?
Did you feel guilty 'cause you're a survivor?
In a crowded room did you feel alone?
Did you call up your mother and tell her you love her?
Did you dust off that Bible at home?

Did you open your eyes and hope it never happened,
Close your eyes and not go to sleep?
Did you notice the sunset for the first time in ages
And speak to some stranger on the street?
Did you lay down at night and think of tomorrow,
Go out and buy you a gun?
Did you turn off that violent old movie you're watchin'
And turn on "I Love Lucy" reruns?
Did you go to a church and hold hands with some stranger,
Stand in line to give your own blood?
Did you just stay home and cling tight to your fam'ly,
Thank God you had somebody to love?

*Refrain Twice*

And the greatest is love,
And the greatest is love.

Where were you when the world stopped turnin'
That September day?

# Why Me? (Why Me, Lord?)

Words and Music by Kris Kristofferson

recorded by Kris Kristofferson


Why me, Lord? What have I ever done
To deserve even one of the pleasures I've known?
Tell me, Lord, what did I ever do
That was worth lovin' you or the kindness you've shown?

*Refrain:*
Lord, help me, Jesus, I've wasted it so.
Help me, Jesus, I know what I am.
But now that I know that I've needed you so,
Help me, Jesus, my soul's in your hand.

Try me, Lord, if you think there's a way
I can try to repay all I've taken from you.
Maybe, Lord, I can show someone else
What I've been through myself on my way back to you.

*Refrain Twice*

Jesus, my soul's in your hand.

# Will the Circle Be Unbroken

Words and Music by Eddy Arnold

recorded by Johnny Cash

There are loved ones in the glory
Whose dear forms you often miss.
When you close your earthly story
Will you join them in their bliss?

*Refrain:*
Will the circle be unbroken
By and by, by and by?
In a better home awaiting
In the sky, Lord, in the sky.

In the joyous days of childhood
Oft' they told of wondrous love
Pointed to the dying Savior,
Now they dwell with Him above.

*Refrain*

You can picture happy gath'rings
'Round the fireside long ago.
And you think of tearful partings
When they left you here below.

*Refrain*

# You Are My Sunshine

Words and Music by Jimmie Davis and Charles Mitchell

recorded by Duane Eddy and various other artists

The other night dear as I lay sleeping,
I dreamed I held you in my arms.
When I awoke dear I was mistaken,
And I hung my head and cried:

*Refrain:*
You are my sunshine, my only sunshine,
You make me happy when skies are gray.
You'll never know dear how much I love you.
Please don't take my sunshine away.

I'll always love you and make you happy,
If you will only say the same.
But if you leave me to love another
You'll regret it all someday:

*Refrain*

You told me once dear you really loved me,
And no one else could come between.
But now you've left me and love another,
You have shattered all my dreams.

*Refrain*

# You Decorated My Life

Words and Music by Debbie Hupp and Bob Morrison

recorded by Kenny Rogers

All my life was a paper,
Once plain, pure, and white,
Till you moved with your pen,
Changin' moods now and then
Till the balance was right.
Then you added some music,
Ev'ry note was in place;
And anybody could see all the changes in me
By the look on my face.

*Refrain:*
And you decorated my life,
Created a world where dreams are a part.
And you decorated my life
By paintin' your love all over my heart.
You decorated my life.

Like a rhyme with no reason
In an unfinished song,
There was no harmony,
Life meant nothin' to me
Until you came along.
And you brought out the colors,
What a gentle surprise;
Now I'm able to see all the things life can be,
Shinin' soft in your eyes.

*Refrain*

# You Don't Know Me

Words and Music by Cindy Walker and Eddy Arnold

from the film *Clambake*
recorded by Eddy Arnold, Mickey Gilley, Elvis Presley and various other artists

You give your hand to me, and then you say hello.
I can hardly speak, my heart is beating so.
And anyone can tell you think you know me well,
But you don't know me.

No, you don't know the one who dreams of you at night
And longs to kiss your lips and longs to hold you tight.
To you I'm just a friend, that's all I've ever been,
But you don't know me.

*Refrain:*
For I never knew the art of making love,
Though my heart ached with love for you.
Afraid and shy, I let my chance go by,
The chance that you might love me too.

You give your hand to me, and then you say good-bye.
I watch you walk away beside the lucky guy.
You'll never never know the one who loves you so;
No, you don't know me.

*Repeat Refrain and Last Verse*

You'll never never know the one who loves you so;
No, you don't know me.

# You Got It

Words and Music by Roy Orbison, Jeff Lynne and Tom Petty

recorded by Roy Orbison


Ev'ry time I look into your loving eyes,
I see a love that money just can't buy.
One look from you, I drift away.
I pray that you are here to stay.

*Refrain:*
Anything you want, you got it.
Anything you need, you got it.
Anything at all, you got it, baby.

Ev'ry time I hold you I begin to understand.
Ev'rything about you tells me I'm your man.
I live my life to be with you.
No one can do the things you do.

*Refrain*

Anything you want,
Anything you need,
Anything at all.
Doo doo doo doo doo doo.
Doo doo doo doo doo doo.
Doo doo doo doo doo doo.

I'm glad to give my love to you.
I know you feel the way I do.

*Refrain*

Anything at all, baby.
You got it!

# You Had Me from Hello

Words and Music by Skip Ewing and Kenny Chesney

recorded by Kenny Chesney

One word, that's all you said.
But somethin' in your voice calls me to turn
    my head.
Your smile just captured me.
And you were in my future, far as I could
    see.
And I don't know how it happened, but it
    happened still.
You ask me if I love you, if I always will.

Well, you had me from hello.
I felt love start to grow
The moment that I looked into your eyes.
You owned me. It was over from the start.
You completely stole my heart,
And now you won't let go.
I never even had a chance, you know.
You had me from hello.

Inside I built a wall so high around my heart,
I thought I'd never fall.
One touch, you brought it down,
The bricks of my defenses scattered on the
    ground.
And I swore to me I wasn't gonna love again.
The last time was the last time I let
    someone in.

But you had me from hello.
I felt love start to grow
The moment that I looked into your eyes.
You owned me. It was over from the start.
You completely stole my heart,
And now you won't let go.
I never even had a chance, you know.
You had me from hello.

That's all you said.
Somethin' in your voice calls me to turn
    my head.
You had me from hello.
You had me from hello.
Girl, I've loved you from hello.

# You Needed Me

Words and Music by Randy Goodrum

recorded by Anne Murray

I cried a tear, you wiped it dry.
I was confused, you cleared my mind.
I sold my soul, you bought it back for me
And held me up and gave me dignity.
Somehow you needed me.

*Refrain:*
You gave me strength to stand alone again
To face the world out on my own again
You put me high upon a pedestal
So high that I can almost see eternity.
You needed me. You needed me.

And I can't believe it's you, I can't believe it's true.
I needed you and you were there
And I'll never leave. Why should I leave?
I'd be a fool
'Cause I've finally found someone
Who really cares.

You held my hand when it was cold.
When I was lost, you took me home.
You gave me hope, when I was at the end,
And turned my lies back into truth again.
You even called me friend.

*Refrain*

# You Win Again

Words and Music by Hank Williams

recorded by Charley Pride and various other artists

The news is out, all over town,
That you've been seen a-runnin' 'round.
I know that I should leave, but then,
I just can't go, you win again.
This heart of mine could never see
What ev'rybody knew but me.
Just trusting you was my great sin.
What can I do, you win again.

I'm sorry for your victim now,
'Cause soon his head like mine will bow.
He'll give his heart but all in vain,
And someday say, you win again.
You have no heart, you have no shame,
But take true love and give the blame.
I guess that I should not complain.
I love you still, you win again.

# You're the Reason God Made Oklahoma

Words and Music by Sandy Pinkard, Larry Collins, Boudleaux Bryant and Felice Bryant

recorded by David Frizzell & Shelly West

There's a full moon over Tulsa.
I hope that it's shinin' on you.
The nights are gettin' colder in Cherokee
  country.
There's a blue norther passin' through.
I remember green eyes and a rancher's
  daughter,
But remember is all that I do.
Losin' you left a pretty good cowboy
With nothin' to hold on to.
Sundown came and I drove to town
And drank a drink or two.

*Refrain:*
You're the reason God made Oklahoma.
You're the reason God made Oklahoma
And I'm sure missing you,
And I'm sure missing you.

Here the city lights outshine the moon.
I was just now thinking of you.
Sometimes when the wind blows, you can
  see the mountains
And all the way to Malibu.
Everyone's a star here in L.A. County.
You ought to see the things that they do.
All the cowboys down on the Sunset Strip
Wish they could be like you.
The Santa Monica freeway
Sometimes makes a country girl blue.

*Refrain*

I worked ten hours on a John Deere tractor,
Just thinkin' of you all day....
I've got a calico cat and a two-room flat
On a street in West L.A.

*Refrain*

# Your Cheatin' Heart

Words and Music by Hank Williams

recorded by Hank Williams and various other artists

Your cheatin' heart will make you weep,
You'll cry and cry and try to sleep.
But sleep won't some the whole night through,
You're cheatin' heart will tell on you.

*Refrain:*
When tears come down like fallin' rain,
You'll toss around and call my name.
You'll walk the floor the way I do,
Your cheatin' heart will tell on you.

Your cheatin' heart will pine someday,
And crave the love you threw away.
The time will come when you'll be blue,
You're cheatin' heart will tell on you.

*Refrain*

# Artist Index

# Songwriter Index

**Hal David**
121 It Was Almost Like a Song

**Jimmie Davis**
204 You Are My Sunshine

**Jimmy Dean**
24 Big Bad John

**Maribeth Derry**
101 I Can Love You Like That

**Lewis Calvin DeWitt**
67 Flowers on the Wall

**Steve Diamond**
101 I Can Love You Like That

**Dean Dillon**
43 The Chair
150 Ocean Front Property

**Bob DiPiero**
15 American Made

**Stephen H. Dorff**
107 I Just Fall in Love Again
185 Through the Years

**Michael Dulaney**
192 The Way You Love Me

**Holly Dunn**
56 Daddy's Hands

**Ronnie Dunn**
33 Boot Scootin' Boogie
168 She's Not the Cheatin' Kind

**John Durrill**
44 Charlotte's Web

**Melvin Endsley**
169 Singing the Blues

**Don Everly**
108 ('Til) I Kissed You

**Phil Everly**
196 When Will I Be Loved

**Skip Ewing**
208 You Had Me from Hello

**Donna Fargo**
84 The Happiest Girl in the
    Whole U.S.A.

**Dick Feller**
173 Some Days Are Diamonds (Some
    Days Are Stone)

**Keith Follese**
192 The Way You Love Me

**Fred Foster**
144 Me and Bobby McGee

**Dallas Frazier**
63 Elvira

**Snuff Garrett**
44 Charlotte's Web

**Larry Gatlin**
12 All the Gold in California

**Barry Gibb**
120 Islands in the Stream

**Maurice Gibb**
120 Islands in the Stream

**Robin Gibb**
120 Islands in the Stream

**Bob Gibson**
8 Abilene

**Don Gibson**
103 I Can't Stop Loving You
151 Oh, Lonesome Me
179 Sweet Dreams

**Jerry Gillespie**
60 Do You Love as Good as
    You Look
174 Somebody's Knockin'

**Artie Glenn**
54 Crying in the Chapel

**Wally Gold**
124 It's Now or Never

**Randy Goodrum**
36 A Broken Hearted Me
194 What Are We Doin' in Love
209 You Needed Me

**Al Gore**
58 Diggin' up Bones

**Marv Green**
14 Amazed

**Merle Haggard**
23 Big City
73 From Graceland to the
    Promised Land
152 Okie from Muskogee

**Tom T. Hall**
85 Harper Valley P.T.A.

**John Hartford**
77 Gentle on My Mind

**John Hathcock**
193 Welcome to My World

**Dick Heard**
129 Kentucky Rain

**Don Hecht**
188 Walkin' After Midnight

**Don Henry**
199 Where've You Been

**Larry Herbstritt**
107 I Just Fall in Love Again

**Bob Hilliard**
34 Bouquet of Roses

**Dean Holloway**
23 Big City

**Wayland Holyfield**
49 Could I Have This Dance

**Bob House**
49 Could I Have This Dance

**Jewell House**
149 My Son Calls Another Man Daddy

**Harlan Howard**
37 Busted
39 Call Me Mr. In-Between
89 Heartaches by the Number
104 I Fall to Pieces
117 I've Got a Tiger by the Tail

**Marcus Hummon**
51 Cowboy Take Me Away

**Ivory Joe Hunter**
99 I Almost Lost My Mind

**Debbie Hupp**
205 You Decorated My Life

**John Hurley**
175 Son-of-a-Preacher Man

**Alan Jackson**
45 Chattahoochee
200 Where Were You (When the
    World Stopped Turning)

**Mark James**
13 Always on My Mind

**Waylon Jennings**
80 A Good Hearted Woman

**Billy Joel**
166 Shameless

**Archie Jordan**
121 It Was Almost Like a Song

**Merle Kilgore**
160 Ring of Fire

**Tom Petty**
207  You Got It

**Sandy Pinkard**
27  Blessed Are the Believers
211  You're the Reason God Made
      Oklahoma

**Royce Porter**
150  Ocean Front Property

**Elvis Presley**
139  Love Me Tender

**Leroy Preston**
146  My Baby Thinks He's a Train

**Hugh Prestwood**
176  The Song Remembers When

**Curly Putman**
55  D-I-V-O-R-C-E
82  Green Green Grass of Home
86  He Stopped Loving Her Today
147  My Elusive Dreams

**Eddie Rabbitt**
109  I Love a Rainy Night
129  Kentucky Rain

**Mike Reid**
138  Lost in the Fifties Tonight (In the
      Still of the Nite)

**Bud Reneau**
42  Chains

**Smokey Rogers**
79  Gone

**Fred Rose**
30  Blue Eyes Crying in the Rain

**Lee Ross**
148  My Shoes Keep Walking Back
      to You

**Johnny Russell**
9  Act Naturally

**Patti Ryan**
137  Lookin' for Love

**Phil Sampson**
110  I Loved 'em Every One

**Harlan Sanders**
118  If Drinkin' Don't Kill Me (Her
      Memory Will)

**Mark D. Sanders**
106  I Hope You Dance

**Don Schlitz**
70  Forever and Ever, Amen
76  The Gambler
87  He Thinks He'll Keep Her
105  I Feel Lucky
197  When You Say Nothing at All

**Aaron Schroeder**
124  It's Now or Never

**Ronnie Scott**
123  It's a Heartache

**Troy Seals**
138  Lost in the Fifties Tonight (In the
      Still of the Nite)

**Pebe Sebert**
153  Old Flames (Can't Hold a Candle
      to You)

**Martie Seidel**
51  Cowboy Take Me Away

**Lyndia J. Shafer**
11  All My Ex's Live in Texas

**Sanger D. Shafer**
11  All My Ex's Live in Texas

**Billy Sherrill**
147  My Elusive Dreams

**Tia Sillers**
106  I Hope You Dance

**Gloria Sklerov**
107  I Just Fall in Love Again

**Stephony E. Smith**
125  It's Your Love

**John Martin Sommers**
182  Thank God I'm a Country Boy

**Karen Staley**
128  The Keeper of the Stars

**Jack Stapp**
46  Chattanoogie Shoe Shine Boy

**Even Stevens**
109  I Love a Rainy Night

**Redd Stewart**
32  Bonaparte's Retreat
180  Tennessee Waltz

**Mike Stoller**
178  Stand by Me

**Harry Stone**
46  Chattanoogie Shoe Shine Boy

**Nat Stuckey**
58  Diggin' Up Bones

**Chip Taylor**
16  Angel of the Morning

**Wayne Thompson**
13  Always on My Mind

**Sonny Throckmorton**
113  I Wish I Was Eighteen Again
132  The Last Cheater's Waltz

**Aaron Tippin**
198  Where the Stars and Stripes and
      the Eagle Fly

**Allen Toussaint**
177  Southern Nights

**Merle Travis**
170  Sixteen Tons

**Travis Tritt**
94  Here's a Quarter (Call Someone
      Who Cares)

**Ernest Tubb**
191  Walking the Floor Over You

**Glenn D. Tubb**
171  Skip a Rope

**Leroy Van Dyke**
20  Auctioneer

**Rafe VanHoy**
22  Baby I Lied
163  Sail Away
195  What's Forever For

**Jon Vezner**
199  Where've You Been

**Cindy Walker**
59  Distant Drums
206  You Don't Know Me

**Steve Wariner**
136  Longneck Bottle

**Don Wayne**
50  Country Bumpkin
162  Saginaw, Michigan

**Jimmy Webb**
38  By the Time I Get to Phoenix

**Cynthia Weil**
93  Here You Come Again

**George David Weiss**
40  Can't Help Falling in Love

# More Collections from The Lyric Library

## BROADWAY VOLUME I

An invaluable collection of lyrics to 200 top Broadway tunes, including: All at Once You Love Her • All I Ask of You • And All That Jazz • Any Dream Will Do • As Long As He Needs Me • At the End of the Day • Autumn in New York • Bali Ha'i • Bewitched • Cabaret • Castle on a Cloud • Climb Ev'ry Mountain • Comedy Tonight • Don't Rain on My Parade • Everything's Coming up Roses • Hello, Dolly! • I Could Have Danced All Night • I Dreamed a Dream • I Remember It Well • If I Were a Bell • It's the Hard-Knock Life • Let Me Entertain You • Mame • My Funny Valentine • Oklahoma • Seasons of Love • September Song • Seventy Six Trombones • Shall We Dance? • Springtime for Hitler • Summer Nights • Tomorrow • Try to Remember • Unexpected Song • What I Did for Love • With One Look • You'll Never Walk ne • (I Wonder Why?) You're Just in Love • and more.

\_\_\_\_\_00240201 ....................................................................................................................................$14.95

## BROADWAY VOLUME II

200 more favorite Broadway lyrics (with no duplication from Volume I): Ain't Misbehavin' • All of You • Another Op'nin', Another Show • As If We Never Said Goodbye • Beauty School Dropout • The Best of Times • Bring Him Home • Brotherhood of Man • Camelot • Close Every Door • Consider Yourself • Do-Re-Mi • Edelweiss • Getting to Know You • Have You Met Miss Jones? • I Loved You Once in Silence • I'm Flying • If Ever I Would Leave You • The Impossible Dream (The Quest) • It Only Takes a Moment • The Lady Is a Tramp • The Last Night of the World • A Little More Mascara • Lost in the Stars • Love Changes Everything • Me and My Girl • Memory • My Heart Belongs to Daddy • On a Clear Day (You Can See Forever) • On My Own • People • Satin Doll • The Sound of Music • Sun and Moon • The rey with the Fringe on Top • Unusual Way (In a Very Unusual Way) • We Kiss in a Shadow • We Need a Little istmas • Who Will Buy? • Wishing You Were Somehow Here Again • Younger Than Springtime • and more.

\_\_\_\_\_00240205 ....................................................................................................................................$14.95

## CHRISTMAS

200 lyrics to the most loved Christmas songs of all time, including: Angels We Have Heard on High • Auld Lang Syne • Away in a Manger • Baby, It's Cold Outside • The Chipmunk Song • The Christmas Shoes • The Christmas Song (Chestnuts Roasting on an Open Fire) • Christmas Time Is Here • Do They Know It's Christmas? • Do You Hear What I Hear • Feliz Navidad • The First Noel • Frosty the Snow Man • The Gift • God Rest Ye Merry, Gentlemen • Goin' on a Sleighride • Grandma Got Run over by a Reindeer • Happy Xmas (War Is Over) • He Is Born, the Holy Child (Il Est Ne, Le Divin Enfant) • The Holly and the Ivy • A Holly Jolly Christmas • (There's No Place Like) Home for the Holidays • I Heard the Bells on Christmas Day • I Wonder As I Wander • I'll Be Home for Christmas • I've Got My Love to ꝑ Me Warm • In the Bleak Midwinter • It Came upon the Midnight Clear • It's Beginning to Look like Christmas ꜱ Just Another New Year's Eve • Jingle Bells • Joy to the World • Mary, Did You Know? • Merry Christmas, Darling ꜽe Most Wonderful Time of the Year • My Favorite Things • Rudolph the Red-Nosed Reindeer • Silent Night • r Bells • The Twelve Days of Christmas • What Child Is This? • What Made the Baby Cry? • Wonderful ꜱtmastime • and more.

\_\_\_\_\_00240206 ....................................................................................................................................$14.95

See our website for a complete contents list for each volume:
## www.halleonard.com

FOR MORE INFORMATION, SEE YOUR LOCAL MUSIC DEALER,
OR WRITE TO:

HAL•LEONARD® CORPORATION
7777 W. BLUEMOUND RD. P.O. BOX 13819 MILWAUKEE, WI 53213

# More Collections from The Lyric Library

## CLASSIC ROCK

Lyrics to 200 essential rock classics songs, including: All Day and All of the Night • All Right Now • Angie • Another One Bites the Dust • Back in the U.S.S.R. • Ballroom Blitz • Barracuda • Beast of Burden • Bell Bottom Blues • Brain Damage • Brass in Pocket • Breakdown • Breathe • Bus Stop • California Girls • Carry on Wayward Son • Centerfold • Changes • Cocaine • Cold As Ice • Come Sail Away • Come Together • Crazy Little Thing Called Love • Crazy on You • Don't Do Me like That • Don't Fear the Reaper • Don't Let the Sun Go down on Me • Don't Stand So Close to Me • Dreamer • Drive My Car • Dust in the Wind • 867-5309/Jenny • Emotional Rescue • Every Breath You Take • Every Little Thing She Does Is Magic • Eye in the Sky • Eye of the Tiger • Fame • Forever Young • Fortress Around Your Heart • Free Ride • Give a Little Bit • Gloria • Godzilla • Green-Eyed Lady • Heartache Tonight • Heroes • Hey Joe • Hot Blooded • I Fought the Law • I Shot the Sheriff • I Won't Back Down • Instant Karma • Invisible Touch • It's Only Rock 'N' Roll (But I like It) • It's Still Rock and Roll to Me • Layla • The Logical Song • Long Cool Woman (In a Black Dress) • Love Hurts • Maggie May • Me and Bobby McGee • Message in a Bottle • Mississippi Queen • Money • Money for Nothing • My Generation • New Kid in Town • Nights in White Satin • Paradise by the Dashboard Light • Piano Man • Rebel, Rebel • Refugee • Rhiannon • Roxanne • Shattered • Smoke on the Water • Sultans of Swing • Sweet Emotion • Walk This Way • We Gotta Get Out of This Place • We Will Rock You • Wouldn't It Be Nice • and many more!

_____00240183 ................................................................................................................$14.95

## CONTEMPORARY CHRISTIAN

An amazing collection of 200 lyrics from some of the most prominent Contemporary Christian artists: Abba (Father) • After the Rain • Angels • Awesome God • Breathe on Me • Circle of Friends • Doubly Good to You • Down on My Knees • El Shaddai • Father's Eyes • Friends • Give It Away • Go Light Your World • God's Own Fool • Grand Canyon • The Great Adventure • The Great Divide • He Walked a Mile • Heaven and Earth • Heaven in the Real World • His Strength Is Perfect • Household of Faith • How Beautiful • I Surrender All • Jesus Freak • Joy in the Journey • Judas' Kiss • A Little More • Live Out Loud • Love Will Be Our Home • A Maze of Grace • The Message • My Utmost for His Highest • Oh Lord, You're Beautiful • People Need the Lord • Pray • Say the Name • Signs of Life • Speechless • Stand • Steady On • Via Dolorosa • The Warrior Is a Child • What Matters Most • Would I Know You • and more.

_____00240184 ................................................................................................................$14.95

## COUNTRY

A great resource of lyrics to 200 of the best country songs of all time, including: Act Naturally • All My Ex's Live in Texas • All the Gold in California • Always on My Mind • Amazed • American Made • Angel of the Morning • Big Bad John • Blue • Blue Eyes Crying in the Rain • Boot Scootin' Boogie • Breathe • By the Time I Get to Phoenix • Could I Have This Dance • Crazy • Daddy's Hands • D-I-V-O-R-C-E • Down at the Twist and Shout • Elvira • Folsom Prison Blues • Friends in Low Places • The Gambler • Grandpa (Tell Me 'Bout the Good Old Days) • Harper Valley P.T.A. • He Thinks He'll Keep Her • Hey, Good Lookin' • I Fall to Pieces • I Hope You Dance • I Love a Rainy Night • I Saw the Light • I've Got a Tiger by the Tail • Islands in the Stream • Jambalaya (On the Bayou) • The Keeper of the Stars • King of the Road • Lucille • Make the World Go Away • Mammas Don't Let Your Babies Grow up to Be Cowboys • My Baby Thinks He's a Train • Okie from Muskogee • Ring of Fire • Rocky Top • Sixteen Tons • Stand by Me • There's a Tear in My Beer • Walkin' After Midnight • When You Say Nothing at All • Where the Stars and Stripes and the Eagle Fly • Where Were You (When the World Stopped Turning) • You Are My Sunshine • Your Cheatin' Heart • and more.

_____00240204 ................................................................................................................$14.95

See our website for a complete contents list for each volume:
**www.halleonard.com**

FOR MORE INFORMATION, SEE YOUR LOCAL MUSIC DEALER,
OR WRITE TO:

# HAL•LEONARD®
## CORPORATION

7777 W. BLUEMOUND RD. P.O. BOX 13819 MILWAUKEE, WI 53213

Prices, contents and availability subject to change without notice.

# More Collections from The Lyric Library

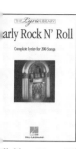

## EARLY ROCK 'N' ROLL

Lyrics to 200 top songs that started the rock 'n' roll revolution, including: All I Have to Do Is Dream • All Shook Up • At the Hop • Baby Love • Barbara Ann • Be-Bop-A-Lula • Big Girls Don't Cry • Blue Suede Shoes • Bo Diddley • Book of Love • Calendar Girl • Chantilly Lace • Charlie Brown • Crying • Dancing in the Street • Do Wah Diddy Diddy • Don't Be Cruel (To a Heart That's True) • Earth Angel • Fun, Fun, Fun • Great Balls of Fire • He's a Rebel • Heatwave (Love Is like a Heatwave) • Hello Mary Lou • Hound Dog • I Walk the Line • It's My Party • Kansas City • The Loco-Motion • My Boyfriend's Back • My Guy • Oh, Pretty Woman • Peggy Sue • Rock and Roll Is Here to Stay • Sixteen Candles • Splish Splash • Stand by Me • Stupid Cupid • Surfin' U.S.A. • Teen Angel • A Teenager in Love • Twist and Shout • lk like a Man • Where the Boys Are • Why Do Fools Fall in Love • Willie and the Hand Jive • and more.

\_\_\_\_00240203  .................................................................................................................................$14.95

## LOVE SONGS

Lyrics to 200 of the most romantic songs ever written, including: All My Loving • Always in My Heart (Siempre En Mi Corazon) • And I Love Her • Anniversary Song • Beautiful in My Eyes • Call Me Irresponsible • Can You Feel the Love Tonight • Cheek to Cheek • (They Long to Be) Close to You • Could I Have This Dance • Dedicated to the One I Love • Don't Know Much • Dream a Little Dream of Me • Endless Love • Fields of Gold • For Once in My Life • Grow Old with Me • The Hawaiian Wedding Song (Ke Kali Nei Au) • Heart and Soul • Hello, Young Lovers • How Deep Is the Ocean (How High Is the Sky) • I Just Called to Say I Love You • I'll Be There • I've Got My Love to Keep Me Warm • Just the Way You Are • Longer • L-O-V-E • Love Will Keep Us Together • Misty • Moonlight in Vermont • More (Ti Guardero' Cuore) • My Funny Valentine • My Heart Will Go on (Love Theme from 'Titanic') • She • Speak Softly, Love (Love me) • Till • A Time for Us (Love Theme) • Unchained Melody • Up Where We Belong • We've Only Just Begun hat the World Needs Now Is Love • When I Fall in Love • Witchcraft • Wonderful Tonight • You Are the Sunshine ly Life • You're the Inspiration • You've Made Me So Very Happy • and more!

\_\_\_\_00240186  .................................................................................................................................$14.95

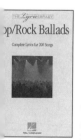

## POP/ROCK BALLADS

Lyrics to 200 top tunes of the pop/rock era, including: Adia • After the Love Has Gone • Against All Odds (Take a Look at Me Now) • Always on My Mind • Amazed • And So It Goes • Baby What a Big Surprise • Ben • Breathe • Change the World • Come to My Window • Do You Know Where You're Going To? • Don't Cry Out Loud • Don't Fall in Love with a Dreamer • Don't Let Me Be Lonely Tonight • Easy • Feelings (?Dime?) • Fire and Rain • From a Distance • Georgia on My Mind • Hero • I Hope You Dance • Imagine • In the Air Tonight • Iris • Just My Imagination (Running Away with Me) • Killing Me Softly with His Song • Laughter in the Rain • Looks like We Made It • My Heart Will Go on (Love Theme from 'Titanic') • New York State of Mind • The Rainbow Connection • Rainy Days and days • Sailing • She's Always a Woman • Sing • Sunshine on My Shoulders • Take Me Home, Country Roads • s in Heaven • There You'll Be • Time After Time • Vision of Love • The Way We Were • Woman in Love • You're nspiration • You've Got a Friend • and more.

\_\_\_\_00240187  .................................................................................................................................$14.95

See our website for a complete contents list for each volume:
### www.halleonard.com

FOR MORE INFORMATION, SEE YOUR LOCAL MUSIC DEALER,
OR WRITE TO:

HAL•LEONARD® CORPORATION

7777 W. BLUEMOUND RD. P.O. BOX 13819 MILWAUKEE, WI 53213

Prices, contents and availability subject to change without notice.